Rainbow Shekinah
Granny

Richard Fellows

WordWyze Publishing

Copyright © 2019 by Richard Fellows

GRANNY RAINBOW SHEKINAH

All rights reserved.

First Published 2019

Richard Fellows reserves the moral right to be identified
as the author of this work.

Short extracts and brief quotations,
may be copied for non-profit personal use only, without prior permission.

Otherwise, no part of this publication may be reproduced,
stored in a retrieval system, or transmitted in any form or by any means,
electronic, mechanical, photocopying, scanning or otherwise,
without the prior written consent of the author.

Cover Photos: Granny: © LJSphotography / Dreamstime.com

Landscape: © Weerapong Worranam / Dreamstime.com

Rainbow: Designed by Freepik.com

Cover Design: Bettina Kradolfer

Co-Published by: WordWyze Publishing – WordWyze.nz

Most Scripture references are from the New King James Version. Copyright ©
1982 by Thomas Nelson, Inc. Used by permission. All rights reserved.

Printed Soft-cover edition: ISBN 978-0-648-58832-0

Epub Edition: ISBN 978-0-648-58833-7

"She is Tree of Life to those who embrace her;
happy are those who hold her."
(Proverbs 3:18)

"Can a mother forget the baby at her breast,
and have no compassion
on the child she has borne?
Though she may forget, I will not forget you."
(Isaiah 49:15)

DEDICATION

To Bettina, you are a faithful friend, one that stands through the years. The people God brings across my paths are usually lifesavers. When we crossed paths a number of years ago, that season of hanging out was life-restoring, so much fun and joy. Thank you so much for your hours of graphic work on my book covers, you bring a book alive. You are truly gifted from Above, my friend. I honour you. God bless.

Dedicated to you, God, for as You say,
"For who finds Me, finds life." (Proverbs 8:35)

FOREWORD

It is with great respect for my friend, Richard Fellows, that I write this foreword for his 2nd book, "Granny Rainbow Shekinah". In this inspirational book, Richard boldly tackles the subject of the supernatural manifestation of the Triune Godhead and His angelic host in this terrestrial world and in the affairs of human history.

It is because of Richard's quest to know the truth; his desire to understand the veiled; and his deep relationship with the Lord, that he has had the confidence to explore this subject and present his findings to us.

During the days of the early Church, it must have been reasonably common and accepted for angels to manifest in a human form to engage, interact with, and help God's people. The writer of Hebrews writes,

"Be not forgetful to entertain strangers, for thereby some have entertained angels unawares." (Hebrews 13:2)

During a revival amongst children in a remote part of India, our community has experienced such a phenomenon. The supernatural appearance of accurately positioned people during times of persecution and the need for comfort, became a natural and welcoming experience for us.

On a number of occasions, members of our family have awoken during the night to see a beautiful senior lady in a physical form, sitting in a chair, feeding one of the babies in our Children's Home a bottle of milk. In the morning, the evidence of helpful activity that had not been undertaken by any one of us, was evident. Babies had been fed, nappies had been changed, and the room had been tidied. Due to a rich atmosphere of God's presence and the helpfulness of these encounters, we just accepted that the Lord was happy to be with us in some way, shape, or form to help us with our daily life.

Living with a community of seers for many years, has revealed to us that heavenly beings in human form may already be interacting with our lives, even though we may be naturally unaware. In towns familiar to us, with a growing Kingdom presence, angels are openly walking streets, making prayers for Kingdom advancement and bringing protection to God's people.

We have come to understand that during seasons of heightened spiritual activity, and as heaven and earth unite together with increasing glory, that the supernatural manifestation of heavenly beings in human form, is an absolutely normal activity of the Kingdom of God on the earth.

The Gospels share with us that when Jesus was being baptised by John in the River Jordan, the heavens opened, and the Holy Spirit descended upon Jesus in the form of a dove and rested upon Him. Does the Holy Spirit only manifest in the form of a dove, or has the Spirit manifested in other forms, throughout the pages of the Bible? Is the Holy Spirit still taking on different forms today?

Combining Biblical Scholarship with historical and current testimony, Richard gives us a greater understanding of who the "Granny," feeding our babies a bottle, may be!!!

My suggestion is that as you read this book, you keep alongside you an open Bible, as well as an open mind. Let the Scriptures speak for themselves and enlighten you. Let the testimonies and questions presented, increase your curiosity, understanding, and expectation. May faith arise within you to open the way for higher levels of Kingdom activity to be attracted to your life.

Jason Cobb

The Life Foundation, New Zealand.

Contents

DEDICATION v
FOREWORD vii
PREFACE xiii
CHAPTER 1 - He is Closer than You Think 15
CHAPTER 2 - Created in OUR Image and Likeness! 21
CHAPTER 3 - Celestial Bodies of Glory 29
CHAPTER 4 - The Holy Spirit Like a Rainbow 47
CHAPTER 5 - Jesus in Disguise 59
CHAPTER 6 - He Veils His Face for Glory 69
CHAPTER 7 - Shekinah Appears as an Old Woman 75
CHAPTER 8 - Granny Rainbow Shekinah! 91
CHAPTER 9 - What You Did to the Least; You Did to Me 103
CHAPTER 10 - The Men in White Linen 109
CHAPTER 11 - Mystical Marriage and Heavenly Jewellery 119
CHAPTER 12 - Concluding Appeal 129
REFLECTIVE SCRIPTURES 139
BIBLIOGRAPHY 145

PREFACE

This book was birthed from encountering a number of divine appearances of God in human likeness. There was a season in New Zealand where a number of us encountered these appearances, to the point that it could not be denied or said that we imagined it. We were encountering God in disguise. This book may be stretching for some, but as you read, we will reveal step by step that Scripture and history records that God has, many times, appeared in human likeness and in disguise (Mark 16:12). If He did it in the Old Testament (Genesis 32:24-30), and Jesus did it in the New Testament (John 20:14), then why should we be shocked that God could appear in disguise and walk amongst us today?

Many in history, and to the present day, have had visions and appearances of Jesus turning up in physical form. But what if Jesus also transforms into a beggar or a stranger and walks amongst us, passing us in the street and giving aid to those who are in need (Hebrews 13:2 – entertain messengers)? Are our hearts aware of this possibility, or is this too unbelievable? There are accounts of this in history. What if Jesus' Sermon of "What you did for the least of these, my brethren, you did for Me," also included ministering to Jesus in disguise, and him ministering to us (Matthew 25:40)?

When one studies the Godhead (or the Trinity), it is easy to get into diagrams and labels, like drawing a Triangle on the board to capture the concept. But does this really help us in asking "Who is the Godhead" and what "forms" do they exist in, if they are persons? Open just about any Systematic Theology book on the subject of the Trinity, and you will find very little, if any, on "what is the actual nature of God?" Does the Father have an eternal form? Does the Son have an eternal form? If so, does the Holy Spirit have an eternal form? Is the Godhead just a floating, eternal presence, or does God, the one essence in three persons, have individual celestial bodies of glory? These are some questions we will be answering in this book.

In the Old Testament, there are many occasions of God appearing as a man or as the angel of the Lord in "forms" of theophany. If the Father is the Ancient of Days, and Jesus is the eternal Son of Man, who was born into flesh in the incarnation and took human likeness, then what form or likeness has the Holy Spirit appeared in, throughout history? Is the Holy Spirit, who is God, who is a person, totally different (in form, image and essence) to the other members of the Godhead (Trinity), or in the same likeness? I would assume a similar likeness. Again, these are some more of the questions we will wrestle with throughout the book.

Richard Fellows (2019)

HE IS *Closer* THAN YOU THINK

In the divine encounters that many of us have experienced, it was revealed to us that the Holy Spirit appeared (not as incarnation, but a kind of morphing, a transforming) in the form and likeness of an old lady, who often rode on a scooter. Wherever this old woman would appear, undeniable supernatural wonders would happen, expressing beautiful Kingdom love.

In Chapter Eight, we will read about these encounters. You might be reading this and thinking, what heresy is this? Has this author lost the plot? I don't believe I have, and I have documented that there is early Jewish and Rabbinical agreement that they believed the Spirit of Glory, the *Shekinah*, did at times appear (morph) as an old woman and sometimes as a princess. This *Shekinah* glory is a visible manifestation of God on earth, whose presence is portrayed through a natural occurrence. The word *Shekinah* is a Hebrew word meaning "dwelling" or "settling". It refers to the dwelling or settling of the Divine Presence of God.

Before we totally dismiss these ideas, we need to examine the roots of our faith. Also, these ideas and historical claims predate any mystic or Kabbala tradition, which were picked up on later in history. By saying this, I am *not* saying that the Holy Spirit's gender is female; I *am* saying the Holy Spirit has appeared, and can appear in the "form" of a female. It is not that God is male or female, but that He has all the attributes that made us, both male and female, in His image. Most will go so far as to agree at this point. He has appeared in "bodily form" like a spiritual dove (through the veil) at Jesus' baptism. (Luke 3:22)

The early Christian Apologist Tertullian (210 AD) said,

> "You would have been refuted in this matter by the Gospel of John when it declares that the Spirit descended in the body of a dove and sat upon the Lord.

When the said Spirit was in this condition, He was truly a dove as He was also the spirit. Nor did He destroy His own proper substance by the assumption of an extraneous substance."[1]

When the Scriptures say that the Holy Spirit remained on Jesus (John 1:33), this does not mean a dove was on Jesus for three and a half years. It means that many saw the Holy Spirit descend in bodily form like a dove, which then clothed Jesus as He rested on him.

The Bible doesn't state a gender, but that doesn't mean the dove had to be male or even genderless. Could the Holy Spirit have morphed into a *female* dove? Similarly, Jesus spoke of wanting to gather his children, through the drawing of the Spirit, as a hen gathers her chicks under her wings (Matt 23:37).

There are many accounts in Rabbinic texts and Jewish folklore about visions or encounters with the Shekinah, the Spirit of Glory - woman at the wall (in 4 Ezra 9:38-10:24, dating from around the first century. Midrash Tehillim 106; Kav ha- Yasher, chap 93, Otzar ha-Ma asiyot, in Pesikta Rabbati).

Throughout the Chapters of this book, we will cover topics such as, what is the image and likeness of God? Does God appear in human likeness? What is the nature of the eternal Godhead, and how has this 'Being' revealed Himself in creation? Does the Godhead have eternal celestial bodies of glory? What is the Holy Spirit's 'form' and likeness? What is the 'form' of the Rainbow – the Spirit of Glory? And why does the Holy Spirit veil His face?

---

[1] David W. Bercot, *A Dictionary of Early Christian Beliefs*, Hendrickson Publishers, Inc., 1998, p.344.

We will also look at appearances of Jesus, in the Bible and throughout history, in disguise; The Holy Spirit as the Shekinah, and appearances as an old woman in human form (not incarnation), based in Jewish theology, and in Church history of the Saints. Then, we'll look at modern encounters of 'Granny Rainbow'; The Great Cloud of Witnesses; the Men in white linen, and entertaining strangers; Moses and Elijah in the transfiguration; and Mystical Marriage and Heavenly Jewellery in the history of the Church. Then lastly, we will look at who is Lady Wisdom…

The reader will be happily surprised that I include a large amount of Scripture and take the reader step by step, building my Thesis to explain the phenomena.

In Mark 1:14-15, Jesus said that the Kingdom of God was at hand. This was to awaken us to the fact that we are to turn towards the Kingdom realm, and know that this Kingdom and the Host of heaven, the Godhead and the angels, as well as the Great Cloud of Witnesses, are as close as our hand is to our body. The Kingdom is present in us and beside us. Jesus said that He would never leave us or forsake us, and I believe He is closer than we could ever imagine.

> *'Now, after John was put in prison, Jesus came to Galilee, preaching the gospel of the kingdom of God, saying, 'The time is fulfilled, and the kingdom of God is at hand. Repent and believe the gospel'." (Mark 1:14-15)*

Jesus even said of the Holy Spirit that He would dwell with us, beside us and in us, looking at us and speaking in us by His voice. Dwelling like a shadow, His presence ever near us, so that we would not be orphans,

> *"And I will pray to the Father, and He will give you another Helper, that he may abide with you forever, "the Spirit of truth,*

whom the world cannot receive, because it neither sees Him nor knows Him; but you know Him, for He dwells with you and will be in you. "I will not leave you orphans; I will come to you." (John 14:16-18).

It is the Holy Spirit who strengthens us, and His eyes run to and fro throughout the earth, looking for whom He can comfort and strengthen. He moves behind the veil and also morphs in human likeness. The Holy Spirit is present everywhere (omnipresent), and He can appear in multiple locations at once. Appearing (making oneself known and visible) is different to just being present.

"That He would grant you, according to the riches of His glory, to be strengthened with might through His Spirit in the inner man." (Ephesians 3:16)

"For the eyes of the Lord run to and fro throughout the whole earth, to show Himself strong on behalf of those whose heart is loyal to Him." (2 Chronicles 16:9)

"The eyes of the Lord are on the righteous, and His ears are open to their cry." (Psalm 34:15)

God is closer than you think, open your heart to the possibility that Jesus and the Holy Spirit often appear in visible form on the earth and walk amongst us. Be strengthened that you are never alone, and God is always watching you, and strengthening you to bring you to His Heavenly Kingdom.

"And the Lord will deliver me from every evil work and preserve me for His heavenly kingdom. To Him be glory forever and ever. Amen." (2 Timothy 4:18)

We end this chapter with the words of the early Church Father Irenaeus, in his works, *Against Heresies*,

> "With Him [God] were always present the Word and Wisdom, the Son and the Spirit, by whom and in whom, free and spontaneously, he made all things, to whom also he speaks, saying, 'Let Us make man in our image and likeness'."[2]

---

[2] St. Irenaeus of Lyons, Against Heresies, Book IV, Chapter 20.

CREATED IN OUR

Image

AND LIKENESS

When it comes to thinking about the Holy Spirit, we need to start right at the beginning. What is the Holy Spirit's nature, what does Scripture reveal about this member of the Godhead? Many Theologians have debated, throughout history, what the image of God is like, and what this term means. In this chapter, we will not be battling through these deep debates. But we will zone in on a number of passages to reveal some essential truths and descriptions. Just to clarify, the title of this chapter refers us being made in God's image – "our image" comes from Genesis.

Genesis 1 is the first occurrence in Scripture in revealing the nature and likeness of God's image,

> *"Then God said, let us make man in our image, according to Our likeness; ... So, God created man in His own image, in the image of God He created him; male and female He created them." (Genesis 1:26-27)*

In verse 26, the word for God is "Elohim," which is plural, meaning more than one is being spoken of. Then in verse 27, it changes into a singular term for God (His). Therefore, the text is saying, let us (more than one) create man in our image, in *His* (singular) image…. God is one, but more than one person (we would say, three persons). Theologians often caution that one must not just assume the doctrine of the Trinity from only Genesis 1:26-27. Therefore, we will build upon this theme in this chapter.

What we are told clearly, is that Man (collective noun), as in male *and* female, are created to image God's likeness. To be human is to reflect/represent God in some way. Therefore, if we assume the Trinity is presented in these verses, then the Holy Spirit has an "Image" and "Likeness" that is interlocked with the other two members of the Trinity. And this image and likeness must reflect somehow in humankind. How it relates completely, is not my point for this chapter. My point is that the Holy Spirit, who is part of "Elohim" in the "Oneness," has His own "Image" and "Likeness," and we could say, a "form" since eternity. The Holy Spirit is not an "it", but a being of personality, with an image and form, capable of will and emotion (Ephesians 4:30).

Now, what I am *not* saying, is that I know exactly what that image and form is, but as a member of the Trinity (Godhead) that co-creates and makes image-bearers, if He wanted to, could He morph into a "likeness" of His image, which reflects as a human?

We know that many times in the Old Testament, God appears as a man. Jacob wrestled with a man who was God; God appeared as the Angel of the Lord; and there are a number of other divine figures that appeared which will be covered in the following chapters. But whichever member of the Godhead appears, this manifestation is a theophany or a morph of the Divine. In these instances, these are not incarnations like Jesus became (Philippians 2:6-7). They were not born in human flesh; they just appeared as humans, morphed like flesh. Just like angels can appear like humans, and not be of human flesh and blood, these theophanies are celestial spirit bodies that can "shape-shift" and manifest in human likeness.

If the Holy Spirit appears as hovering over the waters (Genesis 1:2), as a Pillar of Fire (Exodus 13:21), as a dove (Luke 3:22), could He also manifest, throughout history, in the "image" and "likeness" that other members of the Godhead have? We will come back to this idea, as Jewish thought and Church history have said, 'yes'!

In the following passages, we will look and see that each member of the Trinity (Godhead) is revealed in Scripture, first in the Old Testament and then in the New.

Another passage that uses plural pronouns for God is Genesis 3:22. After Adam and Eve sinned, God laments - that "man has now become one of us" (mim-men-nū), knowing good and evil.

In Isaiah 48:16, the speaker says, "The Lord God has sent Me, and His Spirit." Many Theologians claim that the spokesman of the verse is the second member of the Godhead, based on verse 12, where He identifies Himself as the "First and the Last" - a name Jesus claims in John's book of Revelation. If this is correct, then all three Persons are linked together in this verse. For those that don't know, Theologians usually affirm the second member to be the Eternal Son.

> *"Come near to Me, hear this, I have not spoken in secret from the beginning. From the time that it was, I was there. And now the Lord God and His Spirit have sent Me." (Isaiah 48:16)*

You have Lord God (Father - Yahweh), His Spirit (Holy Spirit – Ruach) and Me (the Son - Jesus/Yeshua) the complete Godhead.

In Isaiah 61:1, the Lord God and the Spirit of the Lord are said to be upon the one who speaks. What is interesting about this verse is that in Luke 4:18, Jesus reads it and says He is the one being anointed. The Father has anointed Jesus (the eternal Son) with the Holy Spirit who has come upon Him.

> *"The Spirit of the Lord God is upon Me because the Lord has anointed Me." (Isaiah 61:1)*

The Lord (Father), is pouring out His Spirit (the Holy Spirit) upon Me (Son).

Isaiah 63 is another passage that reveals all three members of the Godhead.

> *"I will mention the lovingkindnesses of the Lord and the praises of the Lord, according to all that the Lord has bestowed on us, and the great goodness toward the house of Israel, which He has bestowed on them according to His mercies, according to the multitude of His lovingkindnesses. For He said, Surely, they are My people, children who will not lie. So, He became their Saviour. In all their affliction He was afflicted, and the Angel of His Presence saved them. In His love and in His pity, He redeemed them; And He bore them and carried them all the days of old. But they rebelled and grieved His Holy Spirit."* (Isaiah 63:7-10)

You have the Lord, the Angel of His Presence, and the Holy Spirit being revealed.

We will now look at the evidence from the New Testament on the Holy Spirit being unique from the Father and the Son (Jesus). The New Testament reveals that the Holy Spirit is God, He comes from the Father, He is sent by the Father and Son, and that He speaks and comforts people on earth.

> *"But Peter said, 'Ananias, why has Satan filled your heart to lie to the Holy Spirit and keep back part of the price of the land for yourself? While it remained, was it not your own? And after it was sold, was it not in your own control? Why have you conceived this thing in your heart? You have not lied to men but to God."* (Acts 5:3-4)

> *"But when the helper comes, whom I shall send to you from the Father, the Spirit of truth who proceeds from the Father, He will testify of Me."* (John 15:26)

> *"But the Helper, the Holy Spirit, whom the Father will send in My name, He will teach you all things, and bring to your remembrance all things that I said to you." (John 14:26)*

> *"The Spirit of truth, whom the world cannot receive because it neither sees Him nor knows Him, but you know Him for He dwells with you and will be in you. I will not leave you orphans; I will come to you." (John 14:17-18)*

It is interesting that in John 14:17, it says the Holy Spirit can be known, and He dwells close to us and in us. When the passage says the "world" cannot see Him or know Him, that does not mean He can't be seen or known. The Holy Spirit can be "seen and known", but not to those whose eyes are not spiritually regenerated and open. Keep this thought in mind as you read through each chapter of this book.

In the New Testament, we often see the words, "He," then "Holy Spirit". But that does not mean that the Holy Spirit cannot morph into a reflection of the "image" and "likeness" of male or female. For male and female are both part of the image of God.

It's interesting to note that God is identified by the name YHVH (Yahweh), known as the Tetragrammaton. The masculine and feminine elements are perfectly balanced in the Tetragrammaton. The 'yod' has a masculine meaning, the 'heh' a feminine one, and the 'vav' a masculine character.

Conclusions: What I am and am *not* saying

In this chapter, we have looked at the "Oneness" of "Elohim" and the nature and likeness of the Godhead. In doing that, I am *not* saying God is a human, and I'm *not* saying God is a particular gender. What I **am** saying is the Trinity (Godhead) created mankind in the image and likeness of Their image. What this totally consists of, no one knows, but we are told God has an expression of an "image" and "likeness" that reflects in us. Therefore, God from eternity has a form and an image, even if the Godhead does not reveal it fully. If this is not the case, God does not exist, as God must consist of an essence. We have also seen, that many times God has appeared in human likenesses that are different from the incarnation of Jesus. So, I raise the question again, could Holy Spirit appear in human likeness?

CELESTIAL BODIES OF
Glory

In this chapter, we will look at Celestial Bodies of Glory. Scholars often talk of the appearances of the Lord in the Old Testament as Theophanies. A Theophany is a visible manifestation of God's presence. Apart from the Pillar of the Cloud and the Pillar of Fire, most of these manifestations are human-like appearances on earth. These Theophanies, like the Angel of the Lord and such, clearly state in Scripture that they are God.

We could say these manifestations of God, these forms, are Celestial Bodies of Glory. God is revealing Himself in a "form" to unveil His nature and presence. What do I mean by the term "Celestial Bodies"? I mean, God has Heavenly bodies, forms, which they (Godhead) move and appear in. In God revealing His multi-dimensions of His nature, this in no way means that God gains or loses any part of His eternal essence.

John Frame, in his book, *The Doctrine of God,* says,

"The phrases, 'angel of the Lord' and 'angel of God' (even, sometimes, simply angel) often refer to a Divine Being. Not every angel in Scripture is divine; in Revelation 19:10 and 22:9, an angel refuses worship and tells John to worship God instead. But in many cases, the angel is God, and accepts worship. Appearing to Hagar, the angel speaks as God, making covenant with her and her children (Genesis 16:6-13; 21:17-20). In Genesis 22:11-12, the angel tells Abraham that "you have not withheld from me your son, your only son," where "me" must be God (v2). The angel identifies himself as "the God of Bethel," in Genesis 31:11-13 and in Genesis 32:30, Jacob says of the man (called an angel in Hosea 12:4) who wrestled with him, that "I saw God face to face, and yet my life was spared." (See also Genesis 48:15-16; Exodus 3:2-22; 13:21, 14:19; 32:34; 23:20-23; Numbers 20:16; Isaiah 63:8-9; Zechariah 1:8-12; Malachi 3:1). But in Exodus 23:20 and 32:34, God distinguishes

Himself from the angel. The angel is one who God is "sending" (23:20)."³

I believe the eternal God, the three persons of the Trinity revealed themselves to Heaven (before the earth was created) in celestial "forms" of glory. That is out of their "Oneness" they manifested in "Godhead forms" to be interacted with in Heaven and later in creation, "the onlybegotten God, who is in the Father's bosom, has made him known" (John 1:18). Jesus said, "I came out and came forth from God" (John 8:42). Coming out of the "Oneness" comes from the Cappadocian doctrine known as the "Perichoresis" - the doctrine of the ontological interpenetration of persons or mutual co-inherence or indwelling of the persons within the Godhead, thought to be taught by Jesus in his declaration, "The Father is in Me, and I am in the Father" (John 10:38, 14:10, 17:21). Also, the Spirit of truth proceeds from the Father (John 15:26). If we say this is not true, then one must conclude that these personal eternal persons are totally invisible and unknowable. The eternal God can be everywhere (Omnipresent) and still appear in a "form"; this we see in Scripture. This is expressed in Transcendence and Immanence - two characteristics of God – which are a pair. God is both transcendent over and immanent in His creation, that is, God is both beyond the world and in it, but not *of* the world.⁴ If we will accept that God can appear as the Angel of the Lord, as the "Man" Jacob wrestled with, the Angel of His presence, why could these manifestations not start in Heaven first? Or does the invisible in Heaven just appear on earth?

Many Evangelical thinkers will not like the term "Celestial Bodies" referring to God. This is because they say God is spirit and spirits don't have physical bodies. But I am not saying God

---

³ John Frame, The Doctrine of God, P&R Publishers, 2002, p.634

⁴ Norman Geisler, Systematic Theology, Volume Two God/Creation, p. 519

(Trinity/Plural) has physical bodies; I'm saying that God can have spiritual forms (that appear as bodies). And in this, I'm not saying they are finite, created bodies; I'm saying God (Trinity/Three Persons) as an eternal Spirit, who is before all things, can localise a physical appearance (the term physical means "see-able", and not opposite to spiritual substance), without being limited to just that body and location in Heaven and on earth. There is rabbinic literature that accepts the idea that God can have a body in Heaven [5]. Once in the earth's atmosphere, these appearances, theophanies can morph into material substances, as in being clothed in them (matter, terrestrial human likeness).

The commandment against idolatry is not due to God having no divine image. The prohibition of idolatry is about God's jealousy – God does not want us to worship anything/anybody other than who He is. . If we worship a graven image, we are not worshipping HIM, but a man-made representation of what we think He could look like (Exodus 20:5).

It is important to point out what is not meant by the word "Trinity". It does not mean there are three gods (tritheism), or that there are three beings in the Godhead. The Trinity is expressed as a plurality of persons and unity of essence; God is three persons in one nature.

The incarnation is another topic (flesh and blood, not theophany), which we are not talking about here, but we can see in the incarnation, that it is possible for an eternal spirit (God) to dwell fully in a body. Of Jesus, in Colossians 2:9, it says, "For in him the

---

[5] Alon Goshen Gottstein, The Body as Image of God in Rabbinic Literature, and Michael Fishbane, Some Forms of Divine Appearance in Ancient Jewish Thought.

whole fullness of deity dwells bodily". It shouldn't then be hard to believe that the Godhead can have eternal celestial bodies.

Some may say, "but Scripture says God is invisible; at least the Father is, so they can't all have forms". My reply to this is, if Scripture says the Father sits on a throne, He must be visible, so we need to re-interpret the context. When Colossians 1:15 says the Son, "is the image of the invisible God", it is in the context that the Father has not come to earth and revealed Himself here. Not that in Heaven the Father has no form or likeness and must be invisible. He is simply invisible to *our* eyes.

So, we have the eternal God, One yet Three, that manifests their image and form in Heaven in celestial bodies, which can appear on earth in a theophany appearance, morphing into a terrestrial human form. And then there is the incarnation of Jesus, which is different (not the subject of this book).

We see Scripture speak of the Father who had Glory with the Son before the world was created. And the Spirit of Glory was with them also, which is the Holy Spirit. The term "Son of Man" was regarded as a Heavenly and pre-existent being. A good book that deals with this term is *The Pre-existent Son; Recovering the Christologies of Matthew, Mark, and Luke*, by Professor Simon J. Gathercole, who lectures at the University of Cambridge. But for us in this chapter, we will look at passages that reveal divine celestial bodies of the Godhead.

> *"And now, O Father, glorify Me together with Yourself, with the glory which I had with You before the world was." (John 17:5)*
>
> *"No one has ascended to heaven, but He who came down from heaven, that is the Son of Man who is in heaven." (John 3:14)*

> *"And above the firmament over their heads was the likeness of a throne, in appearance like a sapphire stone; on the likeness of the throne was a likeness with the appearance of a man high above it." (Ezekiel 1:26)*

In Heaven, many forms and manifestations of God are revealed, almost multidimensionally. We must not try to make God simple, for He is not. Going by information we all know, Heaven has a throne, so was anyone ever sitting on it before the creation of the earth? I would say so. The Father definitely was. The Holy Spirit also seems to be implied by the Spirit of glory, the rainbow over the throne and the Seven Spirits of God. We even see in Scripture that Jesus can appear in Heaven in different forms, He is the Pre-existent Son, He can transfigure into a Lamb with seven eyes, and into a Lion. Some may not like this, but if this is not true, then can Jesus only encounter one person on earth at a time, or can He be multiple places at once in multiple dimensions?

The Father, in Scripture, is called the "Ancient of Days", and in Daniel 7:9, it says that the Ancient of Days was seated on a throne. Therefore, He must have a form. Also, Daniel 7:13 distinguishes Him from the Son,

> *"I was watching in the night visions, and behold, One like the Son of Man coming with the clouds of heaven. He came to the Ancient of Days, and they brought Him near before Him." (Daniel 7:13)*

In John 3:13, we see that Jesus as the "Son of Man" came down from Heaven, who was previously in Heaven. The Eternal Word, who can manifest in a celestial form in Heaven, who was in Heaven, came down and incarnated in human flesh (form).

> *"And as we have borne the image of the man of dust, we shall also bear the image of the heavenly Man." (1 Corinthians 15:49)*

In Heaven now, He is seen as the gentle Jesus, as Scripture says He will come back as He left. But Scripture also says that in Heaven, He can look like the following,

> *"And having turned, I saw... One like the Son of Man, clothed with a garment down to the feet and girded about the chest with a golden band. His head and hair were white like wool, as white as snow, and His eyes like a flame of fire." (Revelation 1:12-14)*

> *"And I looked, and behold, in the midst of the throne and of the four living creatures, and in the midst of the elders, stood a Lamb as it had been slain, having seven horns and seven eyes, which are the Seven Spirits of God sent out into the earth." (Revelation 5:6)*

Let's recap what we have reflected on,

- When God created Heaven, the "Three persons as One" manifested their presence in a celestial form to interact and reveal themselves. Most of these appearances were in human likeness, in celestial bodies of glory.

- We see in Ezekiel 1:26 — a divine man is seated on the throne which Ezekiel saw. This was not a future prophecy, but an encounter. We see Daniel 7:9 — the Ancient of Days was seated, his garment was white as snow, and his hair like pure wool.

- John 3:13 says the Son of Man was in Heaven before He came to earth.

- These forms in Heaven are eternal spiritual forms, celestial bodies, they are not flesh and blood incarnations, until Jesus is born on the earth as flesh and blood (then we have one).

- The Godhead is eternal, the "Three that are One" are eternal Spirit, this does not change. Manifesting a form or changing forms, is an eternal expression of their eternal Spirit.

Now that we have seen that in Heaven, the Godhead can take on forms of presence, let's have a look at their forms manifesting in creation.

In the Garden of Eden:

"And they heard the sound of the Lord God walking in the garden in the cool of the day, and Adam and his wife hid themselves from the presence of the Lord God amongst the trees of the garden." (Genesis 3:8)

Appearing to Hagar, Abraham's concubine:

"Then the Angel of the Lord said to her [Hagar], 'I will multiply your descendants exceedingly so that they shall not be counted for multitude…' Then she called the name of the Lord who spoke to her, 'You are the God who sees (El Roi), for she said, 'Have I also here <u>seen the back of Him</u> who sees me?'" (Genesis 16:10-13) (emphasis mine)

Appearing as 3 men to Abraham:

Then the Lord appeared to him by the terebinth trees of Mamre, as he was sitting in the tent door in the heat of the day. So he lifted his eyes and looked, and behold, three men were standing by him, and when he saw them, he ran from the tent door to meet them, and bowed himself to the ground, and said, My Lord, if I have now found favour in Your sight, do not pass on by Your servant." (Genesis 18:1-3)

Note that it does not say that the Lord and two others appeared to Abraham. The Hebrew says Yahweh appeared to him, then he lifted his eyes, and saw *3 men*. Nowhere in the whole chapter, does it mention these men being anything other than a manifestation of Yahweh Himself. I believe the whole narration is a view of Yahweh in three persons. The next chapter, Genesis 19, specifically says two angels went to Sodom, which I believe were two angels sent *after* Yahweh's visit with Abraham.

For further study on this topic, you can read Michael S. Heiser's book, *The Unseen Realm, Recovering the supernatural Worldview of the Bible*,[6] and Bogdan G. Bucur's paper, *The Early Christian Reception of Genesis 18: From Theophany to Trinitarian Symbolism*.[7]

Bucur states in his paper,

> "Philo sees in the mysterious guests 'the Father of the universe' (πατὴρ τῶν ὅλω) and his accompanying two powers, the creative (ποιητική) power and the royal one (βασιλική)—in scriptural terms, He-Who-Is (ὁ ὤν), 'God' (θεός) and 'Lord' (κύριος). It is clear, however, that these are not distinct entities, but rather aspects of the one ineffable divinity, and that the alternation between singular ('Lord') and plural ('three men') teaches the

---

[6] Michael S. Heiser, *The Unseen Realm, Recovering the supernatural Worldview of the Bible*, Lexham Press. p 187

[7] Bogdan B. Bucur, *The Early Christian Reception of Genesis 18 from Theophany to Trinitarian Symbolism*

attentive exegete about the higher and lower modes of spiritual perception."

Appearing to Jacob, and wrestling with him:

> "Then Jacob was left alone, and a Man wrestled with him until the breaking of day... So, Jacob called the name of the place Peniel. For I have seen God face to face, and my life is preserved." (Genesis 32:24-30)

Appearing to Moses in the flaming bush:

> "And the Angel of the Lord appeared to him in a flame of fire from the midst of a bush. So, he looked, and behold the bush was burning with fire, but the bush was not consumed... So, when the Lord saw that he turned aside to look, God called to him from the midst of the bush and Moses hid his face, for he was afraid to look upon God." (Exodus 3:2,4)

Appearing to Moses on Mt. Sinai:

> "And when He had made an end of speaking with him on Mount Sinai, He gave Moses two tablets of the Testimony, tablets of stone, written with the <u>finger</u> of God." (Exodus 31:18) (emphasis mine)

Appearing to the 70 elders of Israel, along with Moses and Aaron:

> "And they saw the God of Israel. And there was under <u>His feet</u> as it were a paved work of sapphire stone, and it was like the very heavens in its clarity. But on the nobles of the children of Israel, He did not lay <u>his hand</u>. So, they saw God, and they ate and drank. Then the Lord said to Moses, Come up to Me on the mountain and be there, and I will give you tablets of stone, and

the law and commandments which I have written, that you may teach them." (Exodus 24:10-12) (emphasis mine)

To Moses, after he asked to see God's full glory:

"And the Lord said… 'Then, I will take away <u>My hand</u>, and you shall see <u>My back</u>; but <u>My face</u> shall not be seen." (Exodus 33:23) (emphasis mine)

"Not so with my servant Moses, He is faithful in all My house. I speak to him face to face, even plainly, and not in dark sayings. And he <u>sees the form of the Lord</u>." (Numbers 12:7-8) (emphasis mine)

Appearing to Joshua as an Army Commander, before the battle of Jericho:

"And it happened, when Joshua was by Jericho, he looked up, and he saw a man standing opposite him with his sword drawn in his hand. And Joshua went to him and said, Are you with us, or with our adversaries? And he said, Neither. I have come now as the commander of Yahweh's army. And Joshua fell on his face to the earth, and he bowed down and said to him, is my Lord commanding his servant? The commander of Yahweh's army said to Joshua, 'Take off your sandals from your feet, for the place where you are standing is holy.' And Joshua did so." (Josh 13-15)

* Commander of the army is the Lord, a pre-incarnation of Jesus; a normal angel would not allow one to bow down to him, or call the ground holy where he stood.

Appearing to Gideon in Ophrah:

> *"The Angel of Yahweh came and sat under the oak that was at Ophrah... The Angel of Yahweh appeared to him, Yahweh is with you... And Gideon realized that he was the Angel of Yahweh; and Gideon said, 'Oh, my Lord, Yahweh! For now, I have seen the Angel of Yahweh, face to face.' And Yahweh said to him, 'Peace be with you. Do not fear; you will not die.'"* (Judges 6:11-12,21-23)

It is clear from these verses that people have seen forms of God, the Lord appearing. The Father is the Lord, the Son is the Lord, and the Holy Spirit is the Lord in Scripture.

Jacob wrestled with a man who was God; the Angel of the Lord, who appeared to people, talked as God, and Moses saw God's feet and fingers on the mountain. It is interesting that Scripture uses different Hebrew words for face. There is "Peh" which means "mouth", sound to sound, voice to voice, and there is "Panim" which means physical face.

With Jacob — He saw God's face, that being "Panim", but with Moses speaking face to face, Scripture often uses "Peh". He spoke voice to voice (but not always). In Exodus 33:11, it says Moses spoke face to face, but we know in Exodus 33:20, God says, "You can't see my face". So, there is a seeing of a "form" of God (facial features blurred), and there is also seeing His physical face in detail and features.

In Deuteronomy 4:15, God speaks to Israel through Moses and says, "You saw no form (Temunah) of any kind the day the Lord spoke to You at Horeb out of the fire."

But in Numbers 12:8, it says that Moses speaks face to face (Peh, "mouth," not Panim) and sees the "form" (Temunah) of the Lord.

It seems like we are seeing different persons of the Godhead. There is a man figure, an angel figure, and a "formless" person. Could the formless person be Holy Spirit who does not show his face? When I use the word formless, I don't mean, in NO form at all, but in a human-looking (Pillar) form, without facial features, so far revealed in Scripture. Later, in the following chapters, I will dig deeper on whether the Holy Spirit has ever manifested in human form. But for now, let's just deal with the persons of God; there is the Father, the Son of Man, and the Holy Spirit, which also must appear in some form. He was hovering over the water at creation, and I believe He manifested in the Pillar of Cloud in the wilderness.

> *"And it came to pass, when Moses entered the tabernacle that the pillar of cloud descended and stood at the door of the tabernacle, and the Lord talked with Moses. All the people saw the pillar of cloud standing at the tabernacle door, and all the people rose and worshipped each man in his tent door. So, the Lord spoke to Moses face to face (voice to voice), as a man (a person) speaks to his friend." (Exodus 33:9-11)*

We know in this verse that Moses did not see the Lord's face, because He says in verse 20, "you cannot see my face."

When I read this verse, I believe the "Pillar of Cloud" is the Lord – the Holy Spirit, who is overshadowing a shadow like a veil around the Father. Here we have a "form" of the Holy Spirit. In 1 Corinthians 10:1-4, it says that "all were baptised in the Cloud with Moses", but the Cloud was not the Rock which is Christ.

We also see that it was the Holy Spirit that baptised Jesus. Whether baptising with water from the Cloud or as the Dove, it is the Holy Spirit.

> *"And the Holy Spirit descended in bodily form like a dove upon Him. And a voice came out of heaven which said, 'You are My beloved Son, in You, I am well pleased'." (Luke 3:21-22)*

In Luke 1:35, it says, "the Holy Spirit will come upon you, and the power of the Most High will overshadow you". It is the Holy Spirit that comes with power, as He is the Lord Most High, and as He was the Cloud, it is He who will overshadow us. To me, Exodus 33:9-11, is the Holy Spirit, who veils the Father's image, so His body and face cannot be seen in the Pillar. Here we see the Holy Spirit manifest as a Pillar form.

> *"So, shall it be, while My glory passes by that I will put you in the cleft of the rock, and I will cover you with my hand while I pass by." (Exodus 33:22)*

Verse 14 says God's presence will go with him (Moses); His presence is the Holy Spirit. God says, "I will cover you with my hand while I pass by"; who is passing by? "My Glory" — "I pass by". If the Holy Spirit is the Spirit of glory (1 Peter 4:14), then the presence, the "I" (glory) that is passing is the Holy Spirit who was covering His (the Father's) back and face. A number of rabbinic sources say "His Glory" was a divine figure.

It's interesting to note Song of Solomon 2:14 speaking about the dove (symbol of the Holy Spirit) in the clefts of the rocks,

> *"O my dove, in the clefts of the rock. In the secret places of the cliff, let me see your face..."*

In Exodus 34:5, it says 'The Lord descended "in" the Cloud and stood with him there, and proclaimed the name of the Lord." In this verse, we have someone stepping into the cloud coming down. This, I believe, is another member of the Godhead.

When the glory of God came down on the mountain, it is mentioned as being a thick, heavy cloud (Exodus 19:16). The Hebrew word for 'cloud' or 'covering' is 'chuppah'. The cloud came down and sat like a bridal chuppah, and Moses walked in. The Hebrew understanding of lightning is 'glorified fire'. It is the Holy Spirit in the cloud, the mist that baptises with fire and seals us with His flame in our hearts as part of the bride of Christ.

If we go forward in time to the Transfiguration of Jesus on the Mount, we see that a bright cloud overshadowed them, and suddenly a voice came out of the cloud, saying, "This is My beloved Son, in whom I am well pleased." (Matthew 17:5) Here we have the Father in the Cloud of the Holy Spirit, talking through to the Son and those standing with him (including John).

Clarification: what I have presented above is not in any sense like Mormon Theology. Mormonism teaches that the Father has a body of flesh and bones as tangible as man's; the Son also, but the Holy Spirit has not a body of flesh and bones (they got that last part correct). But as Man is, God once was; as God is, Man may become. Mormonism also teaches that God the Father was once a child and mortal and evolved like us, step by step to become God.[8] – We will NEVER be gods; that is the lie of the serpent.

But of a Biblical Spirit celestial body, one Jewish writer says, what is the appearance of God the Father? God is fire, and His throne is fire, clouds and fog surround Him. His face and cheeks

---

[8] Walter Martin, The Kingdom of The Cults, Bethany House Publishers, 2003, p.236.

are in the image of the spirit, and therefore no man is able to recognise Him [9]. But He has a form and image... A friend's Heavenly encounter describes seeing the Father as, "intense light flooded out from the throne of the Father. A transparent white mist swirled around Him inside the rainbow sphere..."[10]

This is also confirmed by Scripture,

> *"His appearance was sparkling like crystal and glowing....Surrounding the throne was a circle of green light like an emerald rainbow." (Revelation 4:3)*

> *"The Ancient of Days was seated, His garment was white as snow, and the hair of His head was like pure wool. His throne was a fiery flame, its wheels a burning fire." (Daniel 7:9).*

The Father does have a body, but because of the brightness of light that radiates out of Him, He cannot be seen, "Father of light, with whom there is no variation or shadow or turning." (James 1:17)

Conclusions: We have seen that all members of the Godhead have a form and likeness. Many of the members are seen in "forms" in Heaven from the beginning. The Father was on His throne (Daniel 7:9). The Son of Man, was in Heaven before He came down to earth (John 3:13). That is in His celestial body, not His incarnation body. We also see many verses that speak of God appearing in the Old Testament: as one who walked in the Garden (Genesis); as a man who wrestled Jacob (Genesis 32:24-30); Moses saw His feet on the mountain (Exodus 24:10-12); Joshua met a man (God), who was the commander of Yahweh's army (Josh 13-15);

---

[9] Howard Schwartz, Tree of Souls: Mythology of Judaism, Oxford Press, 2004, p.24.
[10] Angela Curtis, Talk with Me in Paradise, Kin & Kingdoms Books, 2019, p.61.

Gideon met a man (God), the angel of the Yahweh which sat under the oak that was at Ophrah (Judges 6:11-12,21-23). We also see appearances of God with a face and without a face.

Again, I raise the question, if these forms of God can appear, could one of them be the Holy Spirit?

THE HOLY SPIRIT
Like a Rainbow

Now, we will look at the image and likeness of the Holy Spirit and how He is revealed in Scripture. To do this, we must first look at the Trinity in the throne room. The three "persons" of the Trinity (the Godhead), the Father, the Son and the Holy Spirit live upon the throne. They have individual "forms" (bodies that occupy location), as divine "persons" in Heaven.

Their eternal nature and transcendent presence uphold and fills all creation (Colossians 1:17 – speaking of Jesus, who is the image of God, but representing the whole Godhead). While being before all things, their natures also manifest in their individual forms, which have location, in bodily (human likeness) movement. In Revelation 3:21, it says that Jesus sits on a throne, and the Father sits on a throne (Daniel 7:9). If Jesus sits on a throne and is a person, then the Father must sit on His throne as a person. If this is true of two of the members of the Trinity, then the Holy Spirit must be upon the throne as a person (or at least His tangible presence) as well. The Holy Spirit is God, a person, He cannot be lower or absent from the throne.

While the Trinity is eternal and transcendent, their manifested "forms" can walk around Heaven, while their presence still fills all things and manifests in other places at once. The Holy Spirit is not a mere force; His presence sits upon the throne swirling around the Father, and manifesting as the Rainbow. In creation, He has also appeared as a Pillar of Fire, a Pillar of Cloud, the Seven Spirits of God, a Dove, and Tongues of Fire, to name a few manifestations.

Lightning and thunder and power also comes from the throne, this again is a representation, manifestation, out-flow of the presence of God – the Holy Spirit.

If the eternal Father has a body (I assume we all agree someone was sitting on the throne from eternity?), and the eternal Son has a body (celestial, before His incarnation), then if the Holy Spirit is God and a person, logic has it, He has a body. So, what body does He take and how does He reveal Himself?

My aim in this chapter, is to make the case that the Holy Spirit's body is manifested in a Rainbow presence, in bodily form. I will start my case, with a testimony of a Heaven encounter, and then build the argument from Scripture.

But first, let's get into the throne room!

> *"You are clothed with glory and majesty, Who covers Yourself with light as with a garment" (Psalm 104:1-2).*

The light, veil, mist, robe, around the throne is the light of the Holy Spirit (Shekinah).

> *"Immediately, I was in the Spirit; and behold, a throne set in heaven, and One sat on the throne. And He who sat there was like a jasper and a sardius stone in appearance; and there was a rainbow around the throne, in appearance like an emerald."* (Revelation 4:2-4)

I believe that the Rainbow over and around the throne is the manifestation of the presence of the Holy Spirit. I also believe there are a number of other Scriptures that confirm this. But, let's first look at a Heaven encounter a friend of mine had,

In the Book, *Talk With me In Paradise* by Angela Curtis, she reveals an encounter of a person, who met the Holy Spirit in Heaven,

"When I opened my eyes, I was no longer in the room. I was on a riverbank in the most magnificent garden. Everywhere I looked was perfect, from the grass to the masses of bright coloured flowers. It was glorious, unlike anything I had ever seen… As I stood absorbing it all, a pillar of coloured light like a rainbow came towards me. Joy and a familiar buzz tingled through my entire body. I recognised that sensation. 'Who are you?' I asked, wondering if the pillar could speak. 'I am a Companion sent by God for you,' a gentle voice replied. 'You asked for me,' He said. Love surrounded me, His power so strong it was audible. Captivated, enraptured, fascinated, that's the only way I can describe it."[11]

Now many will be sceptical of this encounter, but can we use it to give light on Scripture? Can Scripture come alive by this encounter?

We would all agree that the Holy Spirit is God, He is like the Lord, and a person (has personality). He is also called the Counsellor and Convictor in Scripture. 1 Peter 4:14 says that the Holy Spirit is the "Spirit of Glory", meaning He manifests the presence of Glory.

> *"If you are reproached for the name of Christ, blessed are you, for the Spirit of Glory and of God rests upon you…" (1 Peter 4:14)*

Ezekiel 1:28 says, speaking of his vision of the throne,

> *"Like the appearance of a rainbow in a cloud on a rainy day, so was the appearance of the brightness all around it. This was the appearance of the likeness of the glory of the Lord."*

In the Heaven encounter mentioned above, it speaks of "a pillar of coloured light, like a rainbow came towards them". This is very similar to the Pillar of Cloud that was with Moses, in the Wilderness, which I said I believed was the Holy Spirit (Chapter 3)

---

[11] Angela Curtis, Talk With Me in Paradise, Kin & Kingdoms Books, 2019, p.13.

or at least two members of the Godhead interacting in one encounter.

Ezekiel 1:28 says that this appearance was like a bright light rainbow in a cloud, which was the Spirit of Glory. This appearance had the likeness of the Lord, it wasn't the Lord who was sitting on the throne (verse 26), but had the likeness of the Glory of the Lord. Now the Glory of the Lord is a person, it is the Spirit, the Holy Spirit who manifests His presence. Ezekiel is saying there was one like the Lord, but also different, because He was another member of the Godhead. So, is it rational to say, the Holy Spirit can manifest as a Rainbow "form" person?

Isaiah 3:8 says that the Lord's glory has eyes; that glory can see *"Are against the Lord, to provoke the eyes of His glory."* Not that glory has eyeballs, but has sight, is personal.

Scripture also says the Holy Spirit is a Lamp, and this was the brightness in the rainbow. Scripture also says the Holy Spirit comes like rain or water (Joel 2:23-24; Hosea 6:3; John 7:37-39); A Cloud (Exodus 13:21-22); as seven flames, seven lamps (Revelation 4:5). These are all natures, elements that manifest a rainbow.

Ezekiel 8:3 even says the Spirit of glory has a 'form of a hand'…

The Holy Spirit is a person who manifests glory, like a lamp in a cloud on a rainy day, appearing like a rainbow, like seven lamps, seven flames (7 colours of the rainbow), showering spiritual rain into the earth from His presence. We could add He also comes as Wind (John 3:8; 20:22), as Oil (Acts 10:38), a Dove (Luke 3:22), as Living Water (John 7:37-39), and as a Pillar of a Cloud (Exodus 13:21) and Fire (Acts2:3).

Some may be quick to say, these are just symbolic terms used of the Holy Spirit, not real manifestations. But this is not the case, if you study Church history, you will find that many have experienced (seen) these manifestations, even cloven tongues of fire on people's heads that don't burn.[12] Fire in the Old Testament, was an identifier of the presence of God, a visible manifestation of God's glory and essence.[13] The presence of God once got so intense at one of our Church conferences, that it actually physically rained in the building, yet it was not raining outside.

> *"And the Lord went before them by day in a pillar of cloud to lead the way, and by night in a pillar of fire, to give them light; so as to go by day and night. He did not take away the pillar of cloud by day or the pillar by night from the people." (Exodus 13:21-22)*

We see the Pillar of Light; the Holy Spirit is in Heaven, and then forms in the cloud in the day with rainbow glory, and as a Pillar of Fire at night in the wilderness of Israel. We are told He did not take away the pillar. These descriptions also connect to the Holy Spirit in the New Testament. He doesn't leave them as orphans (John 14:18); He will guide them (John 16:13), He will dwell with them (John 14:17), and He will baptise with fire (Matt 3:11). It's interesting to note a flame of fire can flicker rainbow colours. Jesus was also led into the wilderness by the Holy Spirit (Luke 4:1).

Nehemiah says,

> *"You, in Your great compassion, did not forsake them in the wilderness. The pillar of cloud did not leave them by day, to guide them on their way, nor the pillar of fire by night, to light for them the way in which they were to go. You gave Your good spirit to instruct them…" (Nehemiah 9:19-20).*

---

[12] Examples; Azusa Street, William Seymour, Maria Woodworth-Etter meetings!
[13] Michael Heisler, The Unseen Realm, Lexham Press, 2015, p. 297.

In Hebrews 13:20, it speaks of the Trinity's everlasting covenant of redemption. The Rainbow in the sky is a sign (symbol) of this covenant (Genesis 9:16) – drawing attention to how the Holy Spirit who saves (through the blood of the Son), manifests as a Rainbow (Person) in Heaven.

Some Rabbis almost went so far as bowing down to the Rainbow in the sky. They didn't see it as a finite creation, but as the Holy Spirit, Shekinah, Rainbow, from the throne shining into creation.[14]

Joseph was given a coat of many colours; this was symbolic of the Spirit's covering, the coat of promise. (Genesis 37:3)

Noah saw a Rainbow at the end of the flood, which signified peace and calmness – Symbolic of the Holy Spirit. (John 14:26-27)

A Rainbow is not just a Rainbow according to Rabbi Joseph Bechor Shor (12th Cent), Rather, it's God showing God's self.

The Jews say, 'Do not expect the Messiah until a Rainbow appears, radiating splendid colours throughout the world. At present, the colours of the Rainbow are dull, serving merely as a reminder that there will not be another flood. But the Rainbow that announces the Messiah will have brilliant colours and be adorned like a bride for her bridegroom. When the Rainbow appears, it will be a sign that God has remembered His covenant with Israel, and that the footsteps of the Messiah will soon be heard[15]. The earth will be filled with the glory of the Spirit of glory – Holy Spirit.

The seven colours of the Rainbow over the throne represent the complete perfect light of God. The Spirit illuminates the 'words of life' that flow from the Father through the Son. The arches of the

---

[14] Howard Schwartz, Tree of Souls: Mythology Of Judaism, Oxford Press, 2004, p.79.
[15] Zohar 1:72b

Rainbow are set above *Aravot,* the highest heaven, and the clouds of the Rainbow surround the throne of glory. Above the Shekinah presence Rainbow, are the wheels of the *Merkavah* (throne).

God said that He would dwell in the thick cloud (swirling cloud - 1 Kings 8:12). *"Clouds and darkness are round about Him; righteousness and justice are the foundation of His throne."* (Psalm 97:2) As the Father sits on His throne, the Holy Spirit clothes around Him, like a cloud veiling Him with glory. The word "darkness" means veil, which hides the full image of the Father. The Holy Spirit, which reigns on the throne, can and does also appear in Heaven as a moving, interacting personal Rainbow Pillar.

This veil is like a garment, like a curtain, and like above, so is the pattern below,

> *"I am dark and beautiful, O you, daughters of Jerusalem, as the tents of Kedar, as the curtains of Solomon."(Song of Songs 1:5)*

I have read many Heaven testimonies of people who have seen the crystal "River of Life" flowing from the throne, to experience, further down the river, that it becomes a Rainbow river of glory. The river of life is the Spirit of glory, the Spirit of God.

The one who is a Pillar of Cloud around the throne, flows out life into the river of life. *Wisdom has built her house, She has hewn out her seven Pillars (Proverbs 9:1).* These Pillars, are the seven colours of the Spirit that flows through heaven as one, cutting, and forming all those that stand in Him. Perfect light flows crystal and unfolds into the coloured Rainbow river of redemption gifts.

From the throne,

> *"She calls from the top of the heights of the City' (Proverbs 9:3)*

Deep calls unto deep,

> *"When you pass through the waters, I will be with you, and through the rivers, they shall not overflow you. When you walk through the fire, you shall not be burned, nor shall the flame scorch you." (Isaiah 43:2)*

When you take a light beam and shine it into a prism, it shatters into seven colours of light like a rainbow. God is perfect light (white light), and when a spirit (human) comes out of eternity and is sent to earth, it is like a child of white light. But once in the earth, our spirit overshadows around our body like a rainbow (aura). The image we reflect, shines through us and around us. As the Father is veiled by the Holy Spirit, so too, are we veiled by the breath of life, the Holy Spirit upholding our spirit to shine through our body. The concept, reality of an aura, does not originate from the New Age movement, but from God.

As in the spiritual (seven colours), so it is in the natural, we are created with seven layers of skin as a covering.

Because the Holy Spirit is omnipresent, at times, streaks of rainbow colours will be seen in the physical world. The Holy Spirit was seen powerfully in Maria Woodworth-Etter's (1844-1924) ministry. One night in Dallas, Texas, while she was preaching, there were seen flames of fire in rainbow colours around her, and a ring of light, having rainbow colours, was seen all around the tent emanating from a pillar of fire.[16]

> *"Arise, shine; For your light has come! And the glory of the Lord is risen upon you. See, darkness covers the earth, and thick*

---

[16] Maria Woodworth-Etter, A Diary of Signs and Wonders, chapter 70.

darkness is over the people, but the Lord rises upon you, and His glory appears over you." (Isaiah 60:1-2)

The Lord once instructed friends of mine to go outside their house and look in the sky. In their campus hovering very low was a single spectacular rainbow coloured cloud. This even caught the attention of the neighbours. The Lord was revealing Himself in a manifestation.

The Jews also believe the Shekinah, the Spirit of Glory, was the Holy Spirit too (Ruach-ha-Kodesh). I think it is reasonable to believe that the Holy Spirit has a celestial body (form). The Jews also believe that the Shekinah has, at times, appeared in a transformed human form on the earth. This we will look at in later chapters.

But we will take this idea step by step. In this chapter, we see that the Holy Spirit has entered into other people's human bodies. In the book of Judges 6:34, in the Hebrew, the verse reads, *"The Spirit of Yahweh clothed himself in Gideon"*. The word "clothed", is the word *"Labash"* and is only used three times in Scripture, Judges 6:34, 1 Chronicles 12:18, and 2 Chronicles 24:20. The word *"Labash"* means to "put on clothes to wear". This verse is saying that the Holy Spirit entered Gideon's body and wore his body and skin like clothes and controlled him. This is a different word than *"hyh"* that just means 'comes upon'.

Jubilee Bible reads, *"And the Spirit of the Lord clothed himself in Gideon."*

Lexham Expanded Bible, reads, *"So, the Spirit of Yahweh took possession of Gideon."*

Net Bible reads, *"The Spirit of the Lord took control of Gideon."*

Conclusions: The Holy Spirit is God, a person, who transcends all creation, but manifests in a celestial form, radiating His presence over the throne. He also walks in Heaven as a bright Rainbow Pillar, with the likeness of the Lord, for He is the image and likeness of God (Genesis 1:26). The Holy Spirit has entered people and taken use of their bodies, as if wearing them like clothes. But, as we will see, the Holy Spirit has also manifested, morphed into his own human likeness form (not incarnation, but transformation).

Jesus
IN DISGUISE

Let's look at the life of Jesus after the Cross and observe His ability to encounter people in disguise and come and go into the earth's atmosphere to visit.

Jesus, after His resurrection, didn't just resurrect as a normal human, but as the God-man in an immortal body. This immortal form gave Jesus the ability to be in many dimensions at once, and also to morph into different human forms. What do I mean by different "human forms"? I mean transfigure into different-looking humans. He came in disguise many times, as we read in Scripture.

We see this in Mark 16:12 and Luke 24:13-16:28 -31, speaking of Jesus,

> *"After that, He appeared in another 'form' to two of them as they walked and went into the country." (Mark 16:12)*

> *"Now behold, two of them were travelling that same day to a village called Emmaus, which was seven miles from Jerusalem. And they talked together of all these things which had happened. So it was, while they conversed and reasoned, that Jesus himself drew near and went with them. But their eyes were restrained so that they did not know Him… Then they drew near the village where they were going, and He indicated that He would have gone farther. But they constrained Him, saying, 'Abide with us, for it is toward evening, and the day is far spent.' And He went in to stay with them. Now it came to pass, as He sat at the table with them, that He took bread, blessed and broke it, and gave it to them. Then their eyes were opened, and they knew Him, and He vanished from their sight." (Luke 24:13-16; 28-31)*

In these two different passages speaking about the same events, we see Jesus walking with these two disciples to a village called

Emmaus. As He walked with them, He was in a different 'form' (The Greek actually uses the word "morphe"), of which they did not recognise, their eyes were closed off from picking up His personality. Jesus was clearly in disguise, and as soon as their eyes were opened, they knew Him and soon after, He vanished out of sight supernaturally. This is not the only place in Scripture that we see this, it happened with Mary Magdalene as she walked away from the empty tomb. She encountered Jesus but did not recognise Him, as she thought He was just the gardener. Jesus had clearly morphed into another 'form' (disguise), had He looked the same as before, He would have had the wounds of the Cross and beatings all over His body, giving Himself away. His face would not have looked like a gardener, and the fact that Jesus spoke to her face to face shows she saw a different face and appearance.

> *"Now, when she had said this, she turned around and saw Jesus standing there, and did not know that it was Jesus. Jesus said to her, Woman, why are you weeping? Whom are you seeking? She, supposing Him to be the gardener, said to Him, Sir, if you have carried Him away, tell me where you have laid Him, and I will take Him away." (John 20:14-15)*

Clearly, for Mary Magdalene to look at Jesus, not knowing who He was, call Him, Sir, and ask Him if He knows where the Lord is (Himself), shows He was in disguise. What is my point in discussing this? My point is, that it is correct to say that after the Cross, Jesus could morph into other human likenesses. He could also visit and encounter people; these visitations I believe still happen today.

Jesus also appeared to Saul (Paul) on the road of Damascus, showing us that, sometime after the Cross, He still encountered people,

"As he journeyed, he came near Damascus, and suddenly a light shone around him from heaven. Then he fell to the ground, and heard a voice saying to him, Saul, Saul, why are you persecuting Me? And he said, 'Who are You, Lord?' Then the Lord said, 'I am Jesus, whom you are persecuting...' And Ananias went his way and entered the house, and laying his hands on him, he said, Brother Saul, the Lord Jesus, who appeared to you on the road as you came, has sent me that you may receive your sight and be filled with the Holy Spirit." (Acts 9:3-5,17)

I believe Saul not only encountered a great light around him from heaven, but Jesus, in that bright light, stood in appearance. He didn't see him, but he was standing there.

From what we have seen in the Scriptures, Jesus is able to visit the earth in visions, appearances and morphing in disguise in human likeness. Throughout history, there have been many accounts of Jesus appearing in disguise, many times as the poor or as a beggar, and then later in the same day appearing as Himself in full glory to reveal that "He" was that person.

Saint Martin of Tours became a Believer at a young age, despite his parents being pagans and not approving. At age 15, he was forced to become a soldier in the Roman army, but he did not want to kill, and suffered for his stand as a Christian. One famous account regarding Martin was the following:

"One very cold winter day, Martin and his companions came upon a beggar at the gate of the city of Amiens. The man's only clothes were rags, and he was shaking with cold. The other soldiers passed by him, but Martin felt that it was up to him to help the beggar. Having nothing with him, he drew his sword and cut his long cloak in half. Some laughed at his funny appearance as he gave one half to the beggar. Others felt ashamed of their own selfishness.

That night, Jesus appeared to Martin. He was wearing the half of the cloak that Martin had given away. 'Martin, still a catechumen (learner), has covered me with this garment,' Jesus said."[17]

Jesus was telling Martin that by caring for the poor he was really caring for Jesus in disguise.

Phillip H. Wiebe in his book, *Visions and Appearances of Jesus*, records two other occasions where Jesus appeared in disguise, the accounts of Gregory the Great and Peter the Banker – 6th Century,

> "A number of ancient accounts describe saints giving gifts to the poor and then being surprised to find that Jesus was the recipient. One of the earliest such accounts is that of Saint Gregory the Great (540 -604), who regularly gave to beggars. One night after Gregory had fed the poor, Jesus appeared to him and said, 'Ordinarily you receive me in the poor that assemble at your board, but today you received Me personally… Some years later a banker, named Peter, is said to have encountered Jesus in the form of a beggar. In 619, Peter had a dream in which his shortcomings were revealed, and as a result, gave away most of his wealth, even giving his coat to a beggar. However, Peter was annoyed when the beggar turned around and sold the coat to someone else. On his way home that day, Peter met Jesus wearing his coat; he commended Peter for his generosity and then disappeared. Peter responded by giving away all his possessions."[18]

---

[17] https://jesusthrumary.blogspot.com/2011/11/nov-11-2011-friday-st-martin-of-tours.html
[18] Phillip H. Wiebe, Visions and Appearances Of Jesus, Leafwood Publishers, 2014, p. 58.

There are also accounts of Jesus appearing in disguise in modern times. For example, as you read this book, someone in the world is encountering Him. These encounters are not always as the poor, sometimes they are strangers who are just at the right place at the right time, divinely, to help. These kinds of accounts make us reflect deeper on Jesus' words in Matthew,

> *" For I was hungry and you gave Me food; I was thirsty and you gave Me drink; I was a stranger and you took Me in; I was naked and you clothed Me; I was sick and you visited Me; I was in prison and you came to Me.'*
>
> *"Then the righteous will answer Him, saying, 'Lord, when did we see You hungry and feed You, or thirsty and give You drink? Or when did we see You sick, or in prison, and come to You?' And the King will answer and say to them, 'Assuredly, I say to you, inasmuch as you did it to one of the least of these, My brethren, you did it to Me.' " (Matthew 25:35-40)*

Yes, we are to love our brethren because Jesus is in them, and yes, we are to love others because they are created in the "image" of God, but we should also love all because that beggar or stranger could be Jesus in disguise. Imagine walking past a stranger in need or a beggar, and thinking they're someone else's problem, then getting to Heaven at the end of your life, and Jesus reveals that it was "Himself" in that form. Oh, Lord, open the eyes of our hearts with Your love, so we do not miss You.

Mother Teresa in her book, *A Gift For God,* presents this idea of seeing Jesus in the stranger, the poor, and the homeless,

> "If sometimes the poor people have had to die of starvation, it is not because God didn't care for them, but because you and I didn't give; were not instruments of

love in the hands of God, to give them that bread, to give them that clothing; because we did not recognise him, when once more Christ came in distressing disguise."[19]

But Jesus doesn't only appear in the suffering or low class, He has been seen morphing and appearing in His traditional description, of robe and sandals and long hair with a beard throughout history. Jesus often also appears as a joyful stranger; whose smile and eyes leave a deep impression of the presence of love that one cannot forget. God does walk amongst us many times in disguise.

Phillip H. Wiebe, in his book just mentioned above, describes many modern and recent accounts people have had with Jesus. Wiebe was a professor of philosophy and taught at Trinity Western University. His research into this topic of Jesus appearing, is considered to be one of the most detailed and scholarly out there. He gave lectures on visions of Jesus from Oxford to Harvard, Chicago to Toronto, and San Francisco to Lublin, Poland. His work is even quoted by the great sceptic and Scholar, Bart Ehrman, who believes his research can't simply be denied.

I will quote a couple of modern encounters with Jesus from Wiebe's book, *Visions and Appearances of Jesus,*

> "Kenneth Logie's life was marked by a number of extraordinary experiences. He was the minister of a Pentecostal Holiness church in Oakland, California, for many years… One Sunday night in April 1954, he again arrived late and, as a result, was still preaching at 9:15, when he saw a shadow on the exterior glass doors, made by someone standing outside. He wondered who might be arriving so late in the evening. He reported that "the

---
[19] Mother Teresa, A Gift For God, , Fount paperback, 1975, p. 32.

door opened up, and Jesus started walking down the aisle just as plain as you are." He turned to the people on one side of the aisle, and then to the people on the other side of the aisle, smiling as he went. He walked up to the platform where Kenneth was preaching, but instead of walking around the pulpit, moved right through it. When He placed his left hand on Kenneth's shoulder, Kenneth collapsed to the floor. Jesus then knelt down alongside him and spoke to him in another language… He says this event was witnessed by the congregation of about fifty people present on that occasion."[20]

Another encounter that happened at the same church,

"Kenneth said when Mrs. Lucero got up to tell her story, she was wearing a black raincoat because the weather had been rainy that day. As she spoke about her vision, she had experienced about a week earlier, she disappeared from view, and in her place stood a figure, believed to be Jesus. He wore sandals, a glistening white robe, and had nail prints in his hands – hands that dripped with oil. Kenneth reports that this figure was seen by virtually everyone in the congregation, which he estimated at 200 people."[21]

Michael Ireland tells of Jesus appearing to 72 Nigerian Christian converts from Islam.[22] These people cannot read, yet they have heard the Gospel and believed. The Boko Haram Islamist militants attacked their group, captured 76 of them, and shot the 4 leaders

---

[20] Wiebe, p. 178.
[21] Wiebe, p. 179.
[22] Michael Ireland, *Miraculously Delivered by God, Unable to read Bible.* 2019 https://www.assistnews.net/miraculously-delivered-by-god-unable-to-read-his-word/

after they refused to deny their new faith, and then demanded the widows should deny their faith or watch their children being shot.

"As they agonized together that evening, their excited children came running in, telling their mothers that Jesus had appeared to them and told them all would be well.

"Jesus then appeared to the whole group of 72, and told them not to fear for He would protect them. He said they should not renounce Him but should stay strong, and that He was the Way, the Truth and the Life.

"The next day, the four mothers gave their decision to the militants – they would not deny Christ.

"The militants prepared to shoot the children, who were already lined up against a wall. The youngest was a little girl of four. Suddenly the militants began screaming and clawing at their own heads. Shouting 'Snakes!' they fled the scene, and some of them dropped dead.

"One of the Christian men reached for the gun of a dead militant but the four-year-old put her hand on his arm to stop him. 'You don't need to do that,' she said, 'Can't you see the men in white fighting for us?'"

Could Jesus be walking past you in the street or coming into your café to buy coffee? The answer is a definite Yes, He could be in disguise.

Conclusions: In this chapter, we have seen that Scripture uses the terms "different form" and "appearances" to indicate that Jesus can morph into other people's likeness and image. We have also seen through history that Jesus has turned up in disguise as the poor and suffering, only to reveal Himself later in full glory. And we have also noticed that Jesus has appeared in modern (recent) times, and there are accounts that He still appears today – just do a search on the internet for accounts of Him appearing to Muslims![23]

---

[23] Tom Doyle, DREAMS AND VISIONS: Is Jesus Awakening the Muslim World? (2012)

HE VEILS
His Face
FOR GLORY

We will now look at the Celestial form of the Holy Spirit, and then in the following chapters, we will look at the Holy Spirit appearing in human form. The Holy Spirit is one who veils His face for the glory of the Godhead.

In John 14:17, it says that the Holy Spirit will dwell with us and in us, so that means that He is able to be very near to us. He can be around us, outside us, and in us. If He has an image and a likeness, then His "form" can appear near us.

So, we read,

> *"The Spirit of truth, whom the world cannot receive because it neither sees Him nor knows Him; but you know Him, for He dwells with you and will be in you." (John 14:17)*

The Scriptures tell us that the Holy Spirit was sent by the Father to glorify the Son and to show forth His nature.

> *"However, when He, the Spirit of truth, has come, He will guide you into all truth; but whatever He hears He will speak, and He will tell you of things to come. He will glorify Me, for He will take what is Mine and declare it to you. All things that the Father has, are Mine. Therefore, I said that He will take of Mine and declare it to you." (John 16:13-15)*

The Holy Spirit chooses to veil His face to bring full attention and focus to Jesus! The Holy Spirit is a person, but He does not reveal His face, because it is through the Holy Spirit that we see the face of Jesus, and in the face of Jesus, we see the face of the Father. The Holy Spirit does not reveal His face or focus attention upon Himself, for it is His mission from the Father to declare the Son and focus attention upon Him. His form as the Spirit of Glory, pillar of coloured light as God, is revealed in His manifestation "forms" and in His action of lighting, illuminating up for us the face of God in the face of Jesus.

> *"For it is the God who commanded light to shine out of darkness, who has shone in our hearts to give the light of the knowledge of the glory of God in the face of Jesus Christ." (2 Corinthians 4:6)*

Many believe that at creation, when God said, 'let there be light,' this light was the glory of the Holy Spirit being decreed from the Father, through the pre-existent Son, fashioning creation into existence.

The Holy Spirit veils His face, to unveil Christ so that we can, with unveiled faces, become the image of Christ through the Holy Spirit. The knowledge of the glory is the revelation revealed by the Holy Spirit's portrayal of Christ.

> *"But we all, with unveiled face, beholding as in a mirror the glory of the Lord, are being transformed into the same image from glory to glory, just as by the Spirit of the Lord." (2 Corinthians 3:18)*

The Holy Spirit has a willingness to serve, often unnoticed, without pursuing recognition and without singled-out honour. Though the Holy Spirit is God, He defers honour, to seek to bring about the glory of another. As the Spirit of Glory, He does not seek His own attention.

We see this in evangelism as the Holy Spirit proclaims the Gospel of Christ. Regeneration of the soul is brought by the Holy Spirit, who brings new life in Christ, and Sanctification by the Holy Spirit transforms us into the image of Christ, to be like Christ. The Holy Spirit seeks to magnify Christ.

I have a friend who has the ability to "see" fully in the Spirit and has gained a very close personal relationship with the Holy Spirit.

This friend can actually see the Holy Spirit. He is described as a bright pillar of rainbow colours (this is one of His celestial forms). He does not have a face, but features. In His shimmering colours you can hear a gentle voice, and you can sense His emotions. "…there came a soft gentle voice…" (1 Kings 19:12). His voice you hear in your spirit, but you feel it coming from outside, from the Holy Spirit. This is because He also lives inside us (John 14:17).

I can remember listening to a podcast once, of Ian Clayton from Sons of Thunder Ministries. He spoke about one time in a meeting, the Spirit appeared as a clothed, robed Being beside him. Ian was curious to know who this being was, so he stepped forward and turned his head to the left and peered into the robed and hooded Being. He was stunned when he looked at where there should have been a face. Staring at him was a shimmering, flickering rainbow-coloured head looking at him, but with no facial features. This was the Holy Spirit in a theophany form.

Mike Parson in his book, *My Journey Beyond Beyond,* who has had many Heavenly encounters says of the Holy Spirit,

> "Nowadays I never ask the Holy Spirit to come, or command Him to come, because He is God (I say 'He', but Ruach (breath spirit) is a feminine gender word in Hebrew. And sometimes the Holy Spirit may appear feminine to you. It's not that God is male or female but that He has all the attributes that made us, both male and female, in His image)."[24]

As we have seen, the Holy Spirit has an eternal celestial body, which can morph into forms, of which He can appear behind the

---

[24] Mike Parson, My Journey Beyond Beyond, The Choir Press, 2018, p. 53.

veil to those whose eyes are spiritually open. And He can morph into human form and likeness and appear like one of us.

To many, these appearances may be too "out there" to believe. You may think this is crossing over from sound doctrine to heresy. But I would ask that you sit tight and keep reading because, as we are about to read in the following chapters, the idea of the Spirit of Glory, the Shekinah, the Holy Spirit appearing as a physical woman, is recorded in early Rabbinic texts and Jewish folklore. This idea is not foreign, and there are also accounts in Church history, and in the days we are living in, of this occurring.

Not that I am saying the Holy Spirit is female, but Scripture does reflect a side of God that expresses the female, motherly emotions and comfort,

> *"As one whom his mother comforts, so I will comfort you. And you shall be comforted in Jerusalem." (Isaiah 66:13)*

> *"Can a woman forget her nursing child, and not have compassion on the son of her womb? Surely, they may forget, Yet I will not forget you." (Isaiah 49:15)*

> *"How often I wanted to gather your children together, as a hen gathers her chicks under her wings, but you were not willing." (Matthew 23:37)*

Neil Weber in his book, *Sophia in the Desert*, says,

> "We look to the Father and Son, as servants look to their Masters. We look to the Spirit, as a handmaid looks to her Mistress. As Psalm 123:2 says, 'Like the eyes of slaves on the hand of their masters, like the eyes of a

maid on the hand of her mistress, so our eyes are on I Am."[25]

Conclusions: The Holy Spirit has an image and likeness, that can dwell around us, apart from just being in us. The Holy Spirit chooses to veil His face to reveal and shine forth the glory of Jesus and the Father. The Holy Spirit can appear in a celestial body form, and also, as we are about to see shortly, in the appearance of human form.

---

[25] Neil, Weber, Sophia in the Desert: 40 Days with Wisdom, Independent Publishing, 2018, p.94.

SHEKINAH APPEARS AS AN OLD Woman

We will now reflect on the presence and appearance of the Holy Spirit in Old Testament times and through the lens of Jewish understanding and theology. As we have seen step by step in this book, each member of the Godhead has manifested into a form or likeness, whether in a celestial body of glory in Heaven, a morphing into human likeness on earth, or as with Jesus, in the nature of incarnation. It is in this chapter, that we will address the issue of whether the Holy Spirit has ever appeared in human likeness on earth.

When it comes to thinking about God manifesting Himself, we need to be careful. The Book of Genesis says that God created man and woman in His image (Genesis 1:27). This means that there are qualities of God that manifest stronger in each gender, but both are fully God's image. Who God is, is a mystery, but at times, God does manifest Himself in "forms" to express Himself. In eternity, I do believe the Godhead was truly unique, there being "Three that are One". As One eternal Spirit, but three Persons, these Spirit personalities chose to take on human likeness and genders (or maybe have eternally been these genders, the true blueprint image of God?). We see this all throughout Scripture and some call them theophanies: the "One" who walked in the Garden with Adam and Eve, the Angel of the Lord, the Angel of His Presence, the one in the Burning Bush, The Lord whom Moses encountered on the Mountain. These were God's heavenly forms – manifesting in our world!!!

We are told the Word, the Logos who became Jesus manifested, (lived in a human body) is God. But before Jesus entered the world, I don't believe He was a book (written word), or some impersonal logos. I believe He stepped out of the divine oneness and morphed into a spirit "form" in Heaven. He didn't become anything new; He wasn't created, He just manifested His presence into a "form", a celestial body, the pre-existent Son. The eternal Father, the eternal

Son, and I believe the Spirit of Glory, the Holy Spirit, who was in the oneness of the Godhead (all unique persons) also stepped out into a "form" in Heaven. We covered this ground in Chapter 3, Celestial Bodies of Glory. Maybe the term "Stepped out" is wrong; perhaps I should just say manifested. Theologians have used phrases such as 'eternal generation,' 'eternal begotten,' 'eternal firstborn,' 'possessed me at the beginning,' 'eternal procession,' to explain this thought. Evangelicals hold to the historical beliefs about the Holy Spirit's deity and ministry, including the position that the Spirit proceeds from both Father and Son.[26]

Some may reject this, but if this is not something like it, then we have three impersonal persons, in a oneness that could not be addressed or communicated with by the host of Heaven, before the earth became lived on by humans, and encountered theophanies. I don't see this in Scripture! I see Heaven alive interacting with the Godhead.

It is interesting that in Jewish history, the Spirit of Glory, the Shekinah, was referred to as the Holy Spirit, who was known to be often described with feminine qualities. The Shekinah was also connected to the Pillar of Fire and Rainbow Presence in the Old Testament. Could it be possible that like the other theophanies, manifestations (Angel of the Lord… etc.), the Holy Spirit has morphed into different appearances on earth? That is, "has taken on" a human likeness - "form"?

Jewish tradition retells many reports of sightings of the Shekinah, the Divine Presence, who made *her* home in the Temple before it was destroyed. The Shekinah is often envisioned as a bride

---

[26] Gregg, Allison, Historical Theology; An Introduction to Christian Doctrine, Zondervan, 2011, p.430.

or as an old woman dressed in black, or as a spirit hovering above the wall.

There are many accounts in Rabbinic texts and Jewish folklore about visions or encounters with the Shekinah at the wall. (Midrash Tehillim 106; Kav haYashar, chap 93, Otzar ha-Ma'asiyot)

There is a tale in *Pesikta Rabbati*, of Jeremiah as he was returning to Jerusalem to see the Temple; of encountering Mother Zion, who was lamenting over the children of Israel while they were in exile. As Jeremiah lifted his eyes, he saw a woman dressed in black. He approached the woman and said, "If you are a woman, speak, but if you are a spirit depart at once". And she replied, "I am Mother Zion".[27]

Mother Zion was an early manifestation (morphing) of the Shekinah, who is the mother of Israel, and whose home was the Temple in Jerusalem. An earlier version of this vision of a mourning woman, like that in *Pesikta Rabbati*, is found in 4 Ezra 9:38-10:24 (Apocrypha), dating from around the first century. You may say, 'a mourning woman?' Would the Holy Spirit mourn? Yes, and can be grieved and insulted. (Ephesians 4:30)

Rabbi Abraham, in the Sixteenth Century, encountered the Shekinah at the wall, as an old woman and as a beautiful bride. As he walked to Jerusalem, he prayed to God to reveal a vision of the Shekinah to him. By the time Rabbi Abraham reached Jerusalem, he felt as if he was floating, and when he reached the Western Wall, Rabbi Abraham had a vision there. Out of the wall came an old woman dressed in black, in deep mourning. When he looked into her eyes, he became possessed with grief. It was the grief of a mother who has lost a child, the grief of the Shekinah over the

---

[27] Howard Schwartz, Tree of Souls: Mythology of Judaism, Oxford University Press, 2004, p.46.

suffering of Her children, the children of Israel who are scattered to every corner of the earth. At that moment, he fell to the ground, feeling faint, and had another vision. In this vision, he saw the Shekinah once more, but this time, he saw Her dressed in Her robe woven out of light, and Her joyful countenance was revealed as that of a beautiful bride. Waves of light arose from her face, an aura that seemed to reach out and surround him.[28]

There is another version of this story in *Kav ha-Yashar*, wherein Rabbi Abraham lifts his eyes and sees the shape of a woman on top of the wall, instead of emerging *from* the wall. Upon seeing Her, he fell on his face, cried and wept, Mother, Mother, Mother Zion. As the Rabbi faints, the feminine figure puts Her hand on his face and wipes away his tears, awakening him.[29]

In these two accounts, we see that in the Jewish mindset, the idea of the Holy Spirit morphing into a person, was not an issue. I would say, it is not an idea, but a reality that they did encounter. If you reject these accounts, you still have to be open to the possibility.

In more recent history, a little over 100 years ago, in December of 1917, there is another account of a woman dressed in black, appearing on the Jaffa road. The ANZACs (Australian and New Zealand Armed Corps) had just freed Jerusalem from the clutches of the Ottoman empire. Ian Johnson, in his book *Israel, God & the ANZACs*, writes,

> "In an unusual, but highly prophetic twist, which is recorded in a letter written by a British Soldier (an Aide of General Allenby), to his mother, the young soldier describes how an unknown Jewish woman came out of

---

[28] Schwartz, p.47.
[29] Schwartz, p47.

the city and approached Allenby, saying with tears, 'Where are the boys of the Auckland Mounted Rifles? For they are my sons and I am their mother.' This was a word from God and sealed a prophetic link between Jerusalem and NZ…"[30]

When asked whether this woman could possibly be an appearance of the Holy Spirit, Ian said "I'm sure she may have been. The statement was very prophetic."

In the Talmud, the feminine spirit emerges as the Shekinah, the Spirit of Glory (God). A Targum states, "In the beginning Wisdom the Lord created…" (Targum Neofitit – Commentary on Old Testament). There is a much earlier understanding that whoever 'Wisdom" is, has connections to the Holy Spirit.

In Sirach 24:15, it says, "She (Wisdom) was the smoke of incense in the Tabernacle, her throne in a pillar of clouds." The Jewish literature, from the Second Temple period, says that Wisdom was "Ruach Elohim", the spirit of God who was hovering over the waters at creation.

First-century extra-biblical literature shows Wisdom and the Holy Spirit to be one and the same (Wisdom of Solomon 9:17). Is there more to this woman Wisdom?

Speaking of this figure of Wisdom and its connection to "let us make man"- 2 Enoch 30:8 and Wisdom of Solomon 9:1 say, "By Your Wisdom, you have formed man."

---

[30] Ian Johnson, *Israel, God & the ANZACs*, His Amazing Glory Ministries, 2012, p. 29

Philo[31] referred to the Pillar of Cloud, descending and resting at the entrance of the Tabernacle, as Wisdom. In time, the Pillar of Cloud became known as the Shekinah.

It is interesting that Proverbs 16:15 says that the light of the King's face is life, and His favour is like a cloud. Again, we see the Holy Spirit as a cloud of glory, light, life, and blessing, illuminating the king's face with Glory and showering spiritual rain down to the earth:

> *"In the light of the king's face is life, and his favour is like a cloud of the latter rain." (Proverbs 16:15)*

The Father sits on His throne, with bright light around Him. His breath (the image of his breath male/female) shines through Him and around Him. His life and favour are like a cloud, like a mist; the Holy Spirit around His throne, like a rainbow mist, full of spring (spirit) rain for all creation.

The Gospel of the Hebrews, which was quoted by many early Church Fathers and regarded by many to record the very earliest record of Jesus' life, refers to the Holy Spirit as a mother. This Gospel was read by Greek-speaking Jewish Christians around 150 AD and was not considered Gnostic. One fragment says,

"Even so, did my mother, the Holy Spirit, take me by one of my hairs, and carry me to the great mount Tabor."

Irenaeus (2nd Century bishop in Gaul/France) said, "The Father always had present with Him, the Word and Wisdom, the Son and

---

[31] Philo of Alexandria (c. 20BC – AD50) was a Jewish-Egyptian philosopher of the Hellenistic period, and of the most important Jewish Philosophers of ancient times.

the Spirit, by whom and in whom He made all things, freely and spontaneously."

Clement of Alexandria (3rd century) said that "She" (Holy Spirit) is an indwelling bride.

Jerome (3rd Century) commenting on Psalm 123:3, said, "…and in the text, 'as the eyes of a maid look to the hand of her mistress,' the maid is the soul, and the mistress is the Holy Spirit."

When it comes to these visions and encounters, they range from a broad time span, from the first century to the sixteenth century, and appear in different forms of Judaism. One cannot just say that these are all mystic groups which we don't accept. Also, these appearances were not imaginations; we are told they were visions, encounters, physical forms (a woman), which touched and ministered to others, even wiping away their tears.

A Vision is "seeing" one appear out of the veil of the spiritual realm. They are real celestial bodies, and they can, as they appear, take on human physical form. We are given examples of an old woman, a bride, and a spirit hovering over the wall. In *Pesikta Rabbati*, this woman is in physical form, the Shekinah had morphed into human form. In the phrase, *"If you are a woman, speak, but if you are a spirit depart at once"*, Jeremiah isn't implying that the Shekinah is not the Spirit of Glory, Mother Zion, but wanting to ascertain whether she is *a dead human spirit* or not. In the version of *Kav ha-Yashar*, the Shekinah has again morphed into human form, and even put her hands on a face and wiped human tears away.

Other sources that recall these encounters are Shivhei ha-'Ari in *Sefer Toldot ha-Ari, Emek ha-Melekh 109; Hemdat Yamin 2:4a; Iggerot Eretz Yisrael; Iggerot mi-Tzefat; Midrash Tehillim* on Psalms 11:3; Exodus Rabbah 2:2.

One tradition claims Shekinah became so real to the people, that She appeared in physical form in two major synagogues. As the Jews journeyed, so did Shekinah. Sightings of her were said to have occurred in Italy, Spain, Germany, Poland and Russia. She took care of the sick, the poor, and those who repented from their sins.

Rabbi Shlomo Rabinowitz of Radomsk said, "The Shekinah protects Jews like a mother taking care of her children." (Tiferet Shlomo on Deuteronomy 29:27)

The Talmudic sages saw the Shekinah as a spiritual essence of beauty, and in the Old Testament, women's names often describe the workings of the Holy Spirit.

Dinah Dye, in her book, *The Temple Revealed in Creation*, says,

> "Sarah is the princess, Rebecca is a yoke that ties two together, and Rachel is the prescribed path of learning. Zipporah (wife of Moses) is the heavenly bird; Yocheded (mother of Moses) is the myrrh of the anointing oil. Of Moses' midwives, Pauh is the soothing, calm voice, and Shaphar is the one who beautifies newborn babies. Batsheva (Bathsheba) is the daughter of seven, for the sevenfold Spirit; Elisheva (Elizabeth) is 'my God is seven,' Malkat Sheva (the Queen of Sheba) is the Queen of Seven, and Deborah is the Debir - the Holy of Holies."[32]

If the Spirit of Glory (Ezekiel 1:28, 1 Peter 4:14, Revelation 4:3), the Shekinah, the Holy Spirit glows the presence of the rainbow

---

[32] Dinah Dye, The Temple Revealed in Creation, Foundations in Torah Publishing, 2016, p.131.

colours, and has been known to be feminine in description and is accepted by Jewish thought to have manifested as a woman (in form) on earth, through many centuries, could not the Holy Spirit appear and morph as an old lady today, as we live our lives?

Now, I have not read the book *The Shack*; many people reject it, and it has brought much controversy. It is a made-up story with Biblical ideas that also play with the idea that the Holy Spirit can manifest as a Woman, called "Saraya," on earth. She is an Asian lady who shimmers with light and has the wind flowing through her hair. Now I am not mentioning this book as historical evidence, but to make us reflect on the possibility.

Is it not possible today, that people who are having visions of Jesus, or seeing Jesus turn up to save them in accidents or encounters, could also be encountering the Holy Spirit appearing and helping people, too?

Could the Holy Spirit not morph into a "Granny" riding on a scooter, helping and comforting people? Like a Granny Rainbow!

> *"Let brotherly love continue. Do not forget to entertain strangers, for by so doing, some have unwittingly entertained angels."*
> *(Hebrews 13:1-2)*

The above passage shows that it is possible to encounter those from heaven in physical human form. The word angels can also simply mean messengers from heaven. Just because it says angels, doesn't mean it can never be the Lord or the Holy Spirit, as Angel of the Lord, and the Angel of His Presence were terms used to describe God in the Old Testament. The term is used to describe a heavenly form, not just created angels. Also, the text might say angels, but some people also encounter only one angel not many. In Jewish tradition, the Holy Spirit was an independent angel/messenger (the word 'angel' in both the Hebrew and the Greek means messenger or agent of change) who existed before creation and was co-creator with God. A messenger, a heavenly form, with human likeness (features) existed. We need to get away from thinking an eternal spirit is a force or just a floating consciousness, God is so much more than that.

Dr. Dinah Dye holds a D MIN in Hebraic Studies in Christianity and reaffirms,

> "In Jewish tradition, the Holy Spirit was an independent angel who existed before creation and was co-creator with God."[33]

What is my point in bringing up the term "angel"? It is to highlight that there is a belief that the Holy Spirit has a form, a nature, a body. Let's not get worked up by the term angel, as I am not implying any relationship or likeness to created angels.

One thing that I am *not* saying, is that God is a woman or that the Holy Spirit is a woman, but that the Holy Spirit can *manifest* in that form. If He can manifest in a physical cloud, pillar in the wilderness, and morph into a dove, why not a woman?

It is interesting that when you study this person, "Wisdom", in Scripture, who is portrayed as a lady, there are almost identical similarities with the Holy Spirit. This again opens up more mysteries than this book will address, but we will look at a couple of references.

> *"Her ways are ways of pleasantness, and all her ways are peace. She is a Tree of life to those who take hold of her, and Happy are all who retain her." (Proverbs 3:17-18)* – Peace of God

---

[33] Dye, p142.

passes all understanding, Tree of Life = Eternal Life, Fruit of the Spirit is JOY!

"Exalt her and she will promote you. She will place on your head an ornament of grace. A crown of glory she will deliver you" (Proverbs 4:8-9) – Humble yourself and God will lift you up in due time, God gives us a covering of grace, for His grace is enough for us, his power! God will crown us with glory.

"Does not Wisdom cry out… I traverse the way of righteousness, in the midst of the paths of justice? That I may cause those who love me to inherit wealth, that I may fill their treasuries. The Lord possessed me at the beginning of His way. Before His works of old. I have been established from everlasting." (Proverbs 8:20-23)

God fights for righteousness, we are to love God above all, and those who love him, He fills their treasuries.

"I love those who love me, and those who seek me diligently will find me. Riches and honour are with me, enduring riches and righteousness. My fruit is better than gold, yes than fine gold." (Proverbs 8:17-19). Of God, "You will seek me and find me when you search with all your heart." (Jeremiah 29:13)

"Wisdom calls aloud outside, She raises her voice in the open squares… Turn at my rebuke, Surely I will pour out my spirit on you… Then they will call on me (wisdom), but I will not answer. They will seek me diligently, but they will not find me. Because they hated knowledge and did not choose the fear of the Lord." (Proverbs 1:20,23,28,29).

It is God who rebukes his people, convicts and then pours out his spirit on those who fear Him.

It is interesting that the teaching of the Trinity is found in Jewish *Targumim* (O.T. in Aramaic) and in commentaries such as the *Zohar*. These Jewish sages taught that God appears in the form of three persons of the Godhead, three manifestations or three emanations. Jewish Targumim, read in the synagogues, gave an understanding of the triune nature of God. God was taught as "Three in One" by Rabbis Simon ben Jochai and Eliezer.

The *Zohar* is a book that was written by Rabbi Simon ben Jochai and his son Rabbi Eliezer in the years following the Roman army's destruction of the Temple in Jerusalem in A.D. 70. In the *Zohar*, the following statements about God are made: "How can they (the three) be One? Are they verily One, because we call them One?" "How Three can be One can only be known through the revelation of the Holy Spirit."

Rabbi Eliezar Hakkalir, A.D. 70, taught the doctrine of three distinct beings revealed in the Godhead in his commentary on Genesis 1:1. He wrote:

> "When God created the world, He created it through the Three Sephiroth, namely, through Sepher, Sapher and Vesaphur, by which the Three twywh (Beings) are meant... The Rabbi, my Lord Teacher of blessed memory, explained Sepher, Sapher, and Sippur, to be synonymous to Ya, Yehovah, and Elohim meaning to say, that the world was created by these three names."[34]

---

[34] Pastor Boshoff, Divine prefigurements in the early Jewish understanding of Yahweh, January 2016

As we conclude this chapter, there is one assumption I must destroy. It is easy if one doesn't know their definitions, to label anyone who says God could morph into a female form, as adopting Gnostic theology, that of the *goddess Sophia*. But this charge has no resemblance in world view or definitions. The *goddess Sophia* teaches monism, not theism, and a number of other contradictions. Monism is the idea that God is unknowable, and all reality is one, everything is God. God in the Gnostic system is the "unknown" God, beyond all that is visible or sensible, and any concept of a Father God is rejected or protested as being the evil God.

This is not what I am saying or teaching and has nothing in common. What I am affirming is, if Jesus could appear in disguise, why not the Holy Spirit?

How close can He come? He radiates a swirl of coloured mist around the Father on the throne, He moves like a coloured Pillar in the heavens. He hovered over creation, and breathed into Adam's body shining through like a garment of light.[35] He manifested like a Pillar of Cloud, and a Pillar of Fire. He morphed into "bodily form" like a dove over Jesus' baptism. He enters people like they are a temple or like a hand fits a glove. How close can He come? Have you entertained Him, the Comforter while being unaware? For He will not let you be an orphan.

Conclusions: In this chapter, we have seen that in Jewish thought the Spirit of glory, the Shekinah, the Holy Spirit was believed to have taken on human form as a bride or as an old woman and appeared on occasions. This belief from the first century onwards was not considered blaspheming, and one can trace even further back the belief that the Holy Spirit was thought of as a kind of angel that could morph. We might not like the term

---

[35] Richard Fellows, *Wilderness Like Eden*, (2019), Wordwyze Publishing p. 118.

angel, but this term is not being used to describe a created angel, but in the same likeness as the Angel of the Lord, and other titles, which were considered in the Old Testament names of God. One must be very careful how they read what I am writing, and don't say "he is saying the Holy Spirit is a created angel," for I am not. The term angel is more a description of a messenger who has taken on form. There is a mystery, and there has to be mystery, for how else could God come to earth in disguise, if it was so obvious. Again, I will restate that I don't believe God is a woman or that the Holy Spirit is female, but that the form and gender can be used as a manifestation of the likeness and image of God.

If Jesus can take on human form in disguise and walk amongst us ministering and flowing his presence, is it not possible that the Holy Spirit does so as well? I believe so!

GRANNY Rainbow SHEKINAH!

What would you say if I said that God the Holy Spirit is again visiting the earth in disguise to minister and comfort certain people? Yes, the Holy Spirit is everywhere (omnipresent), and lives in all born again Believers, but He can also manifest in a location in an image and likeness. In this chapter we are not talking about the Holy Spirit appearing in spirit form, but in a physical human form, most commonly as an old lady. The knowledge that the Holy Spirit has been appearing in physical forms (not incarnations, but morphing) came from a trusted hidden Seer, who works behind the scenes, who informed a few of us that this was the case.

These appearances started to happen regularly in an area of close towns in New Zealand. It was pointed out to us that His appearances often were in the form of an old woman on a scooter. You might think this is ridiculous, but all over the North Island, wherever this woman would turn up, supernatural or unusual things would happen. Not always did He look identical each time, but just about always it was in the form of an old lady. There was one time I experienced Him riding on a scooter as an old man (will share my encounter later).

Now we do not need to get hung up on the word "He" when referring to the Holy Spirit. I do not know whether the Holy Spirit has a specific gender, but there is a big difference between "Physical" gender & "Grammatical" gender. The grammatical gender of the word "Spirit" is masculine (Latin), while in the Semitic languages such as Hebrew, Aramaic, and its descendent Syriac, it is feminine, and in the Greek it is neutral.

Hebrews 13:1-2 tells us to always walk in love and embrace strangers, for by doing so some have unwittingly entertained messengers from the other side. It may startle you, but yes, the other side walks with us and amongst us often. But also, God, the Holy Spirit, and even Jesus can morph and walk amongst us.

> *"Let brotherly love continue. Do not forget to entertain strangers, for by so doing some have unwittingly entertained angels (Greek word for - messengers)." (Hebrew 13:1-2).*

The following stories come from people I know and others who have shared their encounters with this woman. I am not going to give the names of these people, but they are well trusted people (most I have met) and others are friends of people I know. I am not giving their names because this subject is controversial. It is "I" who has stepped forward to bring the light on this revelation and take its criticism.

The following stories have all been confirmed to have been the Holy Spirit. Most of the stories happened in New Zealand and a few in other countries (sometimes the same person experiencing the Holy Spirit as they travelled overseas from airport to airport).

> "On my return to India from Australia, my flight was due to take off at 10.15am. Due to delay in traffic, I reached the airport at 9am. When we (friend & I) stood in line at the counter, there were at least 50 people ahead of me; I knew it was not possible to check-in on time. Friend said she was taking her daughter to the toilet as it was a long line. While she was gone, a lady walks up to me, hands me my ticket, collects my luggage and disappears. Friend can witness that she took less than five minutes to come back, and the check-in line had not moved at all. She was shocked that I had my tickets in my hand. My luggage arrived safe and intact."

Talking of morphing, on later revelation, this lady who took the baggage and disappeared had checked in as the person waiting in the line. Not only did the Holy Spirit morph into a lady, but also as the person waiting in the line.

oOo

"I have two new sightings, here in Te Puke, on a mobility scooter wearing a bright pink fleece jacket… I drove past, and she turned and gave me the biggest smile. I couldn't stop giggling. When I looked in the rear mirror, she was gone. The second sighting, I was driving down the road in Te Puke, with the Autistic girl I work with. She was having a massive meltdown, so I was praying and releasing peace over her. Next minute, I had to slam on the brakes as an old granny, dressed in a bright pink track suit, on a mobility scooter (with a sweet orange flag and everything), wheeled out in front of me. She looked at me and smiled as she went by. I got the giggles, then the girl I work with, got the giggles. We laughed all the way to Rotorua, and the peace of God filled the car."

oOo

"Had a friend who was flying in from the Philippines to Sydney. She had been working with Iris Missions. At the airport, my friend tells me, this very tall lady kept appearing everywhere she was, in the toilets, ordering coffee, at every end of the Airport she went, smiling and then disappearing. My friend thought it was rather funny. Then as she boarded her plane, another super large tall lady is behind her."

oOo

"The other night (daughter) was sleeping in a room with a few babies sleeping in it. Our daughter wakes up in the night and sees an elderly woman in the room feeding one of our babies with a bottle. Then the elderly woman disappeared out of sight."

"Can a mother forget the baby at her breast, and have no compassion on the child she has borne? Though she may forget, I will not forget you." (Isaiah 49:15)

There was no elderly woman living in that house, the Holy Spirit had morphed into an elderly woman and was feeding the baby so that the others (the adults who work in the orphanage) could carry on sleeping and gain rest. We see the beautiful heart of the Comforter and Councillor. This woman has earned the name Granny Rainbow!

oOo

"I had an encounter with Grandad Rainbow! I was walking into a Park with a friend and this old man on a mobility scooter drives past. I thought to myself, 'is this the Lord?', jokingly. Then as I stood in the park watching the kids play, I felt the Holy Spirit like a wind come upon me. I was swaying left and right under His presence. I knew God wanted to do something in the park. A month before that, I had tried to contact a friend, from whom I could not get an answer, no replies. But back in the Park, when I turned around, I saw this lost friend of mine, sitting on a bench in the Park. My friend and I went over to talk to him and pray for him. When we finished, a gemstone supernaturally appeared before his feet to encourage him in his walk."

oOo

"So, a friend and I were walking in the mall and this scooter passes us. We just wondered if it was Granny Rainbow. We went into a store and here comes Granny Rainbow on a scooter with a smiley sticker on the back, we turned to be sure, and we heard this deep laugh and chuckle, yes it was her laughing with kids and having fun."

oOo

"God works in strange ways; I was on my 8 km walk and, on the way, I was telling God how I wasn't pleased with things. Worked so hard this year and… Was not being positive. Then this car drives passed me and stops. This old lady gets out and starts telling me how awesome and amazing I am (almost a little nutty), and then tells me God loves me and then drives off."

oOo

"Two Sundays ago, when her husband picked her up from the train station after her work, as is their custom, they went to top up fuel on the way, especially as it's their son's car. That morning, after filling up with fuel, she realised her card wasn't in her wallet, but in a jacket pocket she'd worn the day before. So, she decided to ask the guy at the counter if she could leave her wallet, or anything as a pledge, till she could rush home and get him the money. As she reached the counter and began to explain, a kind old lady from behind her said, I'll pay for it, Sweetheart. How much is that? She paid the $20 and refused to give her phone number or address saying;

someone might need you to pay for them some day. By the time my friend could finish at the counter, and turn around to thank the old lady, she was gone."

oOo

"One day one of our boarders and I went to the park to try to retrieve his quad-copter from a tree. It was quite high up, and he and I were strapping together broom handles together to try and get it out. It was really high, and the pole was leaning over. We prayed that we would find some way to get it out of the tree. Not long after this, a lady came over and was chatting to us. Turns out she was a professional tree climber and was about to go for a run. In my head I am thinking, 'a professional tree climber – really!! What kind of profession is that?' She talked about how she had been doing it for 12 or so years and had rescued cats out of trees etc. Anyway, she said she would go home and get her climbing gear to come and get it. When she returned, she had some rope with weights on the end, and swung it around vertically like a helicopter a few times. Then she let it go and it flew high into the air around the tree branch, and with a bit of a wiggle, it and the quad-copter fell down and the boarder retrieved it."

oOo

"I never expected to meet the Lord in a shopping mall. My prayer has always been to see Him with my physical eyes while still on earth, but never anticipated that it would happen this way. I had an epiphany, the realisation that I didn't need to learn elaborate prayers, beg to experience more of heaven on earth or live longing to have another vision (I'd had glimpses of the afterlife during and after a near death experience.) All I needed was to learn about heaven's Kingdom realm with the wide-eyed wonder of a child. On my way home where a tall pile of to-do lists waited me, I took a breath and asked the Lord, "What would You like me to do?" "Go to the mall," I felt His voice direct, as I was driving by. So, I pulled in and wondered what He had in mind. I walked around looking at the new shops I hadn't seen before. Then my feet started to hurt from my high-heel shoes, so I decided to go to Kmart and find something more comfortable. The peace became even stronger, so I wondered what He was about to do. I took my time looking for some slides to wear for the summer. As I bent over to pick up the right size, a coin dropped out of my bag and rolled along the floor. That was weird because my bag's 30 cm deep; created to carry everything a woman can imagine.

"I picked it up and moved off to make the purchase. As I was walking towards the checkout, I saw a pair of gym shoes, they were perfect. I grabbed them and headed to find the matching pair in my size. When I reached the racks, there was a couple standing in the aisle looking at the items on the opposite side. I caught myself waiting patiently for them to shuffle over, so I could pass. The peace was even stronger there, and I found myself smiling. I heard them talking, "what a wonderful place to shop, look at these prices!" the lady said. She would have been in her early seventies with straight grey hair. It was her voice that made me smile. It was so sweet, and she sounded like she'd never been shopping before. As I bent down to pick up my shoe size, again a coin dropped out of my giant handbag and rolled along the floor, before turning and disappearing under a rack of clothes. I sighed and put my bag and shoes on the floor.

"Did you just hear something fall on the ground?" the man asked behind me. "Yes, a coin," I replied. "We'll help you find it," the lady said, "Oh, no, it's fine, I can get it." As I turned, they were already on the hunt. "It's all right, we'll help you." "Then finders keepers!" I replied. "Oh, no, we don't need it," she said, and they both giggled. I was bewildered. Who wants to help someone find a coin? They crawled along the floor like children on a treasure hunt, following the path the coin had taken. Around the corner they went giggling, where did I know this couple from? I knew I hadn't met them before, but my spirit recognised them, the lady popped up and smiled, walked straight towards me with her hand outstretched holding the coin. She looked at me, almost through me with the biggest cornflower blue eyes I've ever seen. I held out my hand. "Every little bit counts," she said in the cutest voice ever. "Thank you," I said, and they both turned and walked off like they'd just been on an adventure. I stood there knowing I'd had a divine meeting, but not entertaining the idea it could have been Granny Rainbow. That night, I couldn't sleep, so I prayed. "Was that You, today?" – "Yes, that was me, He said."

> *"Or what woman, having ten silver coins, if she loses one coin, does not light a lamp, sweep the house, and search carefully until she finds it?"* (Luke 15:8)

oOo

There are three parables in the Gospel of Luke where God reveals himself as, the Father looking out for his prodigal son, the good Shepherd who finds his lost sheep, and the Woman who finds her lost coin. Parables with a teaching that God seeks to save and encourage those who are feeling afar.

> *"Wisdom cries aloud in the streets, she lifts up her voice in the broad places; she calls at the head of the bustling corners, at the entrances of the gates, in the city, she offers words. Turn at my reproof, behold I will pour out my spirit on you." (Proverbs 1:20-25)*

The old lady's eyes in these encounters pierce through you with the deepest love and purity, so strong and powerful, *"How beautiful you are, my beloved. Oh, how beautiful, Your eyes are doves" (Song of Songs 1:15)* – *"Turn away your eyes from me, for they overwhelm me." (Song of Song 6:5).*

Most of these encounters with this woman are so supernatural that it is not possible that there is no connection. When this woman turns up, the supernatural seems to start happening. The Holy Spirit is dwelling amongst us in more than one way, morphing into human form. As Hebrews 13:1-2 says, *"Do not forget to entertain strangers, for by so doing some have unwittingly entertained angels (messengers of heaven / a heavenly messenger)."*

We even find accounts of this mysterious woman in the lives of the early Church Saints. St. John of the Cross (1591) was once playing a stick game in a deep river and slipped and fell in and sank to the bottom. While he was at the bottom of the river, he saw a beautiful lady who stretched out her hand, but he was too afraid to grasp it. As he started to drown, he suddenly came up and a peasant was standing on the bank with a pole and pulled him in. This mysterious lady who was under the water was never seen again, and never came up.

St. Clement Mary Hofbauer (1820), while he was praying before the altar of St. Joseph, hundreds of people saw a cloud come down and encase him until he completely disappeared. Then slowly a beautiful woman appeared out of the cloud and smiled at the worshippers. Then disappeared and St. Clement appeared again.

Who was this mysterious beautiful lady? Was she Shekinah, the Holy Spirit, who the Jews say appeared as an old woman and sometimes a beautiful princess?

The Church Father Montanus (170), who headed the movement of Montanist, who offered no new doctrinal revelations, but was on the edge, recalls a dream the prophet Priscilla had, "Appearing as a woman clothed in a shining robe, Christ came to me in my sleep: he put wisdom into me."

Conclusions: some may say it's interesting you all had encounters with an old lady, but this could be normal chance events. And I would reply "Yes", as the Holy Spirit moves around in disguise, it is possible to be wrong. But when you have a woman checking in as you at an airport; an old granny on a mobility scooter bringing a car to a halt, manifesting the presence of God's peace throughout the car in need; a tall lady that appears and vanishes wherever you go in an airport; she appears as another old Granny on a scooter laughing with a deep voice, manifesting the joy of the Lord; waking up to an elderly lady in your house feeding your babies and then vanishes; encounter an old man on a mobility scooter and then the presence of God turns up and a gemstone appears at your feet; or an old lady gets out of a car when you're feeling down and yells and shouts "you're awesome and God loves you," and then drives off; an old lady pays your fuel bill, teaching a gospel principle and vanishes; and a lady who just turns up who is a professional tree climber - these encounters don't seem purely normal. And what gives a little more confirmation, is the Holy Spirit revealed it was Him. If you can believe, all things are possible.

WHAT YOU DID

to the Least,

YOU DID IT
TO ME

We will look deeper into the fellowship of serving others, because you could be entertaining God in disguise!

The phrase in Matthew 25:40, which reads, "And the King will answer and say to them, Assuredly, I say to you, in as much as you did it to one of the least of these, My brethren, you did it to Me," should ring in our hearts to seek and serve God deeper. This section of Scripture speaks on so many levels of reality. The question of who is "My Brethren" can be debated, but at the heart of the message is that we love others because we are created in the image of God. We are told to love our neighbour as ourselves; because there is a union of "being in" each other's hearts,

> *"Teacher, which is the great commandment in the Law? And he said to him, You shall love the Lord your God with all your heart and with all your soul and with all your mind. This is the great and first commandment. And a second is like; You shall love your neighbour as yourself. On these two commandments depend all the Law and the Prophets." (Matthew 22:36-40)*

It is in loving God first, with all our mind and heart, that this union of love overflows to others, who reflect the image of God and deserve to be loved too, second to God.

Matthew 5:8 says *"Blessed are the pure in heart for they shall see God"*. In its present context, this verse is talking about the pure of heart who will be granted to see God in heaven, but also on another level, this verse is speaking to us that in loving from a pure heart, we will see God in people.

Mother Teresa said,

> "Our lives are woven with Jesus in the Eucharist, and the faith and the love that comes from the Eucharist

(union with Christ) enables us to see Him in the distressing disguise of the poor, and so there is but one love of Jesus, as there is but one person in the poor – Jesus. We take vows of chastity to love Christ with undivided love; to be able to love Him with undivided love, we take a vow of poverty that frees us from all material possessions, and with that freedom, we can love Him with undivided love, and from this vow of undivided love we surrender ourselves totally to Him in the person who takes His place. So, our vow of obedience is another way of giving, of being loved. And the fourth vow that we take is to give wholehearted free service to the poorest of the poor. By this vow, we bind ourselves to be one of them, to depend solely on divine providence, to have nothing yet possess all things in possessing Christ."[36]

For many, this walk, this faith journey will be too extreme, or might not fit our personal theology, but it stretches our hearts and perspectives to see God in people, and love with all our hearts. To know nothing, but Christ crucified.

Throughout the chapters of this book, we have observed God being seen in human likeness. In the Old Testament, I will admit it is not always easy to decide which member of the Godhead is appearing in human form in each circumstance, but I would say, that the Bible as a whole, shows us that God has walked on the earth in different appearances. Sometimes revealing Himself, and sometimes in disguise at many levels.

---

[36] Mother Teresa, A gift For God, Fount Publishers, 1975, p.44.

Let's read Matthew 25:34-36,

> *"Then the King will say to those on His right, Come, you blessed of My Father, inherit the kingdom prepared for you from the foundation of the world. For I was hungry and you gave Me food; I was thirsty and you gave Me drink; I was a stranger and you took Me in; I was naked and you clothed Me; I was sick and you visited Me; I was in prison and you came to Me."*

Why do I say, "disguised at many levels"? For God comes in theophanies, He morphs into different forms and has entered into an incarnation (Jesus). God also creates people in His image and likeness to reflect Him. When we minister to them, we are ministering to Him. But this is just one dimension of the reality. If the term "My Brethren," is, in fact, speaking about Believers, then Christ (Jesus) the hope of glory, is living inside every Believer. That being true, then as the body of Christ, the Church of Believers, when we minister to each other, we are ministering to Christ for He lives in us.

There is a union of God in us, and us in them (Godhead), we see this in John Chapter 17: 20-26 where Jesus prays for his disciples,

> *"I do not pray for these alone, but also for those who will believe in Me through their word, they all may be one, as You, Father, are in Me, and I in you; that they also may be one in Us, that the world may believe that You sent Me. And the glory which You gave Me I have given them, that they may be one just as We are one; I in them, and You in Me; that they may be made perfect in one, and that the world may know that You have sent Me, and have loved them as You have loved Me. Father, I desire that*

they also whom You gave Me may be with Me where I am, that they may behold My glory which You have given Me; for You loved Me before the foundation of the world. O righteous Father! The world has not known You, but I have known You; and these have known that You sent Me. And I have declared to them Your name, and will declare it, that the love with which You loved me may be in them, and I in them." (John 17:20-26)

John 17:21, says that believers are in the Father, the Son, and the Holy Spirit (the glory) and not only in name, but possession. We are also told in John 17:26 that the love of the Father and Son (and I expect Holy Spirit too) will be in them. We see this in the phase "that the love with which You (Father) loved Me (Son) may be in them, and I (Son) in them."

Ephesians 5:1-2, tells us to be imitators of God,

"Therefore, be imitators of God as dear children. And walk in love, as Christ also has loved us and given Himself for us, an offering and a sacrifice to God for a sweet-smelling aroma."

Colossians 3:3-4, reminds us that, "You died, and your life is hidden with Christ in God. When Christ, who is our life, appears then you also will appear with him in glory." It is Christ living in us, that people must see as we reflect God in imitating His nature of love.

Scripture tells us to love all, because we are created in the image and likeness of God, and we are to love because those in Christ have "Christ" the hope of glory, living in them. And we are to love all because the Godhead walks amongst us in disguise, morphing and appearing at will. To take this verse "Blessed are the pure in heart for they shall see God" to another level, God will reveal

Himself out of His disguise, which is what we have seen in Granny Rainbow.

There are two places in the New Testament that speak of Jesus being a "form". There is Jesus coming in the incarnation in the "form" of God, coming in the likeness of men, fully revealed. And there is Jesus morphing in the likeness of another "form" in disguise.

> *"Let this mind be in you, which was also in Christ Jesus, who being in the form of God, did not consider it robbery to be equal with God, but made Himself of no reputation taking the form (entering into a terrestrial body) of a bond-servant, and coming in the likeness of men. And being found in appearance as a man, He humbled Himself and became obedient to the point of death, even the death of the cross." (Philippians 2:5-8)*

> *"After that, He (Jesus) appeared in another form to two of them as they walked and went into the country. And they went and told it to the rest, but they did not believe them either." (Mark 16:12-13)*

How close God can come to us, depends on our conscious awareness. He reflects in all mankind, He lives in Believers, His Spirit can come upon us, and He can stand right beside us in disguise in a human form. Jesus said, He would never leave us or forsake us. He had to go away in one dimension, that being, not on earth all the time, so that if He was not in our conscious physical awareness (Who can go from His presence? No one!), the Holy Spirit would come and comfort us, and encounter us, in us and face to face – Granny Rainbow.

THE MEN IN
White Linen

Throughout the chapters of this book, we have seen that God can morph into human likeness, Jesus can disguise Himself in different human likenesses, the Holy Spirit can morph into human likeness, and also Angels can morph into human likeness. But there is also another group of "people" who appear on earth in Scripture from Heaven: that being, the Men in white linen. The Men in white linen are an interesting group, as sometimes they are defined as angels, but many times they are distinctly not angels, but Saints of Old, members of the Great Cloud of Witnesses (Hebrews 12).

The Cloud of Witnesses are the Saints of Old that have gone before us, who watch like in a stadium around us in the spirit. They are messengers who can leave heavenly realms and enter the earth to assist. Some may make the charge that, should this is true, if we encounter them, we are talking to the dead. But this is not true. They are in Heaven, alive, with eternal life. To talk to the dead is to channel a spirit through oneself, or call up a dead spirit. Some may say this is just not Biblical, but how do you explain, for an example one of many appearances: Jesus on the mount of transfiguration and having Moses and Elijah appear? This was not a vision, Moses and Elijah appeared on the earth and engaged in conversation.

> *"Now after six days Jesus took Peter, James, and John his brother, led them up on a high mountain by themselves, and he was transfigured before them. His face shone like the sun, and His clothes became as white as the light. And behold Moses and Elijah appeared to them, talking with Him. Then Peter answered and said to Jesus, Lord it is good for us to be here if you wish…" (Matthew 17:1-4)*

The book of Hebrews tells us that in Heaven there is *"the general assembly and Church of the firstborn, who are registered to God the Judge of all, to the spirits of just men made perfect." (Hebrews 12:23)*

> *"Therefore, we also, since we are surrounded by so great cloud of witnesses, let us lay aside every weight, and the sin which so easily ensnares us, and let us run with endurance the race that is set before us." (Hebrews 12:1)*

> *"Let brotherly love continue. Do not forget to entertain strangers, for by so doing some have unwittingly entertained angels (messengers)." (Hebrews 13:1-2)*

There is no way to get around the facts that Moses and Elijah came to earth. Some may say, but all this was before the Cross, so maybe they were in some "Abraham's Bosom" kind of place, but after the Cross this is not possible. But even if they were in Abraham's Bosom, this is not an objection. In the Book of Acts after Jesus' crucifixion we have in Acts 1:10, two men in white apparel that appear, and then in Acts 5:19, we have an angel coming to open the prison doors. Why doesn't the text in Acts 1:10, just say two angels stood there instead of two men in white apparel? Could they be different heavenly members? Who they are, I don't know, but they must have morphed in human likeness from their celestial bodies they had in Heaven.

> *"And while they looked steadfastly toward heaven as he went up, behold, two men stood by them in white apparel, who also said, Men of Galilee, why do you stand gazing up into heaven? This same Jesus, who was taken up from you into heaven, will so come in like manner as you saw him go into heaven." (Acts 1:10-11)*

Now, in the above verse, we do not see the people shouting, "look there are two angels standing here," they just see two men who have appeared. If I am wrong in my interpretation, and they are angels then we clearly have angels who have morphed into human likenesses.

Zechariah reveals another interesting encounter with men from the Kingdom realm,

> *"On the twenty-fourth day of the eleventh month, which is the month Shebat, in the second year of Darius, the word of the Lord came to Zechariah the son of Berechiah, the son of Iddo the prophet. I saw by night, and behold a man riding on a red horse, and it stood among the myrtle trees in the hollow; and behind him were horses; red, sorrel, and white. Then I said, "My lord", what are these? So, the angel who talked with me said to me, 'I will show you what they are." And the man who stood among the myrtle trees answered and said, 'These are the ones whom the Lord has sent to walk to and fro throughout the earth." So, they answered the Angel of the Lord, who stood among the myrtle trees, and said, "We have walked to and fro throughout the earth, and behold, all the earth is resting quietly." (Zechariah 1:7-11)*

Ezekiel Chapter 9:1-4, describes a man in white linen who is commanded to go out and put a spiritual mark on the foreheads of those who are God's people, while the rest were killed,

> *"Then He called out in my hearing with a loud voice saying, "let those who have charge over the city draw near, each with a deadly weapon in his hand." And suddenly six men came from the direction of the upper gate, which faces north, each with his battle-axe in his hand. One man among them was clothed with linen and had a writer's inkhorn at his side. They went in and stood beside the bronze altar. Now the glory of the God of Israel had gone up from the cherub, where it had been, to the threshold of the temple. And He called to the man clothed with linen, who had the writer's inkhorn at his side, and the Lord said to him, "Go through the midst of the city, through the midst of Jerusalem, and put a mark on the foreheads of the men who sigh and cry over all*

the abominations that are done within it… Just then, the man clothed with linen, who had the inkhorn at his side, reported back and said, "I have done as You commanded me." (Ezekiel 9:1-4,11)

In some cases, I think it is clear to see that some references of men appearing are angels, but this does not refute the evidence of the great Cloud of Witnesses being able to appear at times. For there is clear evidence of Moses and Elijah appearing, and also the story of Enoch opens up interesting questions , which we will look at a little later.

In the book of Daniel, I believe the passages reveal that these appearances are angels. Chapter 9:21 speaks of a man called Gabriel who could fly swiftly, and Chapter 10:6-7 speaks of a man clothed in white linen whose face is like lightening, his eyes like torches of fire,

"Now while I was speaking, praying, and confessing my sin and the sin of my people Israel, and presenting my supplication before the Lord my God for the holy mountain of my God. Yes Gabriel, whom I had seen in the vision at the beginning, being caused to fly swiftly, reached me about the time of the evening offering. And informed me, and talked with me, and said, "O Daniel, I have now come forth to give you understanding." (Daniel 9:20 -22).

"Now on the twenty-fourth day of the first month, as I was by the side of the great river, that is, the Tigris, I lifted my eyes and looked, and behold, a certain man clothed in linen, whose waist was girded with gold of Uphaz! His body was like beryl, his face like the appearance of lightning, his eyes like torches of fire, his arms and feet like burnished bronze in colour, and the sound of his words like the voice of a multitude." (Daniel 10:4-6)

In Job, there is a very interesting passage that talks about a spirit form appearing at night before Eliphaz,

> *"Then a spirit passed before my face, the hair on my body stood up. It stood still, but I could not discern its appearance. A form was before my eyes, there was silence, then I heard a voice saying, 'Can a mortal be more righteous than God? Can a man be more pure than his Maker?'" (Job 4:15-17)*

The Gospel of Mark Chapter 16 describes a man clothed in a long white robe in the tomb sharing with the disciples that Jesus was not dead,

> *"But when they looked up, they saw that the stone had been rolled away, for it was very large. And entering the tomb, they saw a young man clothed in a long white robe sitting on the right side; and they were alarmed. But he said to them, 'Do not be alarmed. You seek Jesus of Nazareth, who was crucified. He is risen! He is not here. See the place where they laid him'." (Mark 16:4-6)*

I can remember reading about the Christian Sadhu Sundar Singh, who in 1912, returned from the mountains in Tibet with an amazing story of finding a four-hundred-year-old Christian hermit in a mountain cave. While climbing the mountain, Sadhu Sundar Singh fell and slid before the opening of a cave. It was inside this cave that he met this Christian hermit who was four-hundred years old, called the Maharishi. Sadhu Sundar Singh spent many days in deep conversation with this hermit who was highly spiritual and advanced in the Kingdom.

The Maharishi revealed that he had a global prayer ministry based in a Himalayan cave, where he prays for the world. That he had been living for four-hundred years and would live until the coming of the Lord. The Maharishi has the ability to enter in and out of the veil, coming and going, into the spiritual kingdom, dimensions, realms, and then at times appearing in the world for seasons. I have also heard of people living today who have encountered this Maharishi, he is still living.[37]

There are a number of people like this on the earth, they will not die. Where does one place them in our discussion in this chapter? They are not angels, and they are not part of the great cloud of witnesses, but they almost function as if they are. I think the story of Enoch describes the Maharishi in some context (not all). Enoch was taken by God, but he did not see death. Many believe that Enoch lives in Heaven, but he also has the ability to walk behind the veil for it is death that cuts us off from living on earth.

> *"So, all the days of Enoch were three hundred and sixty-five years. And Enoch walked with God; and he was not, for God took him." (Genesis 5:23-24)*

There is also another group of interesting "beings" that walk to and fro throughout the earth coming in and out from behind the veil. These are mentioned in Zechariah 6:5 as spirits of Heaven,

> *"Then I turned and raised my eyes and looked, and behold for chariots were coming from between two mountains of bronze. With the first chariot, were red horses, with the second chariot black horses, with the third chariot white horses, and with the fourth chariot dappled horses – strong steeds. Then I answered and said to the angel who talked with me, "what are these, my lord?" And the angel answered and said to me, "These are four spirits of heaven, who go out from their station before the Lord of*

---

[37] For further reading about this: Bernhard Koch, The Mystery of the Maharishi of Mt Kailash: Sadhu Sundar Singh meets the over 300-year-old prayer warrior of Christ, Independent Publishing, 2016

all the earth. The one with the black horses is going to the north country, the white are going after them, and the dappled are going towards the south country." Then the strong steeds went out, eager to go, that they might walk to and fro throughout the earth. And He said, "Go walk to and fro throughout the earth." So they walked to and fro throughout the earth. And He called me, and spoke to me saying, "See, those who go toward the north country have given rest to My Spirit in the north country." (Zechariah 6:1-8)

This is an interesting passage, who are these spirits of Heaven, which are also similar to those mentioned in Zechariah 1:8, which talks of those 'sent by the Lord' to go 'to and fro' through the earth, and 'men' on horseback. If all these passages are talking about the same beings, then we have angels, men in white linen, men on horses, and spirits of Heaven being referred to as the same beings. But if they are not all the same beings, the door is open to interpretation.

As one studies the history of the Church, believers through all ages have encountered the Cloud of Witnesses. General Booth who is known for establishing the Salvation Army reported that he had a vision in which he saw the patriarchs, apostles and angels. Then he saw Jesus who rebuked him for his normal, lazy, professing Christian life. It was this experience that set him on fire to start his mission.

In the book, *The Torn Veil; The Story of Sister Gulshan Esther* – Gulshan Esther reports that Jesus and his apostles all appeared to her when she was a devout Muslim, living in Pakistan. She had very little understanding of who Jesus was, and was healed of a crippling sickness she had, and was taught the Lord's prayer by Jesus. From this experience she went on to become a missionary to Pakistan.[38]

Conclusions: If the majority of these passages are talking about angels in human form, then we have angels who can morph into human form, we have Moses and Elijah appearing out of the great Cloud of Witnesses in human form, and we have Saints like the Maharishi and Enoch who have been caught up, and sustained in the Heavens to visit the earth without seeing death.

---

[38] Gulshan Esther, The Torn Veil; The Story of Sister Gulshan Esther, as told to Thelma Sangster, London, Marhsall Pickering, 1992.

MYSTICAL
Marriage
AND HEAVENLY JEWELLERY

In this Chapter, we will be looking at the history and fellowship of mystical union with each member of the Godhead. What do I mean by this? If one studies Church history, many Believers (Saints), have had encounters and fellowship with different members of the Godhead. And many have received physical heavenly gifts and jewellery from Their hands.

In my previous book, *Wilderness Like Eden,* I documented extensively the supernatural phenomenon of gemstones appearing as gifts from Heaven. This phenomenon I documented from a Jewish, Old Testament witness, and from what is recorded in Rabbinical Commentaries. But since the publication of that book, I have discovered new accounts through Church history, of Saints receiving Heavenly Jewellery from members of the Godhead, which I will address in this Chapter.

Throughout Church history, this phenomenon has been related many times to the term "Mystical espousal," which leads to "Mystical Marriage". In these encounters, members of the Godhead, mainly Jesus, appear and give a Heavenly ring or other gifts to the Believer. These rings and jewels are from Heaven and are clearly seen by those who wear them and by others. But sometimes, the rings are only seen by the one who has received them, as they stay behind the veil in spirit, but are always there on the finger.

St. John of the Cross explains the difference between the espousal and the marriage,

> "In the espousal there is only a mutual agreement and willingness between the two, and the bridegroom graciously gives jewels and ornaments to his espoused. But in marriage there is also a communication and union between the persons. Although the bridegroom

sometimes visits the bride in the espousal and brings her presents, as we said, there is no union of persons... Spiritual marriage is incomparably greater than the spiritual espousal, for it is a total transformation in the Beloved in which each surrenders the entire possession of self to the other with a certain consummation of the union of love."[39]

A Dr. Imbert-Gourbeyre once did a historical study and found close to 100 people who had experienced the mystical espousal or mystical marriage. Of these encounters 55 had received the mystical rings.

Lucy of Narni, born in Italy in the early 1500s was once in prayer, and there she was given a vision of Jesus, Angels and other Saints. Jesus then espoused her to himself, placing a mystical Heavenly ring on her finger. We see in these accounts that visions are not imaginations, but encounters through the spiritual veil as Lucy received a physical ring. We also see that the Great Cloud of Witnesses is active, ministering with Jesus.

Phillip H. Wiebe mentions the account of Stephana Quinzani, born in Italy 1457 near Brescia,

> "Christ is said to have appeared to her accompanied by a few Saints... and then espoused himself to her, giving her a ring that was seen by many people. She experienced another encounter sometime later, after renouncing her own will to do the will of God. Jesus appeared to her and said, 'My daughter, since of the love of Me you have generously stripped yourself of your

---

[39] Joan, Carroll Cruz, Mysteries Marvels & Miracles: In The Lives of The Saints, Tan Books, 1997, p. 142.

own will, ask what you will, and I will grant it to you.' Her reply was, 'I desire nothing but yourself, O Lord.' "[40]

Joan Carroll Cruz, in her book, *Mysteries, Marvels, Miracles, in the lives of the Saints*, lists a number of these accounts with mystical Heavenly Jewellery,

> "St. Catherine dei Ricci experienced the mystical espousal. Our Saviour appeared to the saint, radiant with light, and drawing from his own finger a gleaming ring, He placed it upon the forefinger of her left hand, saying, "My daughter, receive this ring as a pledge and proof that thou dost now, and ever shalt, belong to Me. Catherine described the ring as being of gold and set with a large pointed diamond… Since the event took place in 1542, and St. Catherine lived another 48 years after the event, there was still alive a number of people who had seen the ring when witnesses were questioned in 1614." [41]

It is interesting, having seen them myself, that jewels manifest from Heaven with the same experience: that of the jewellery (ring) gleaming as if glowing with glory on it. I have seen many gemstones appear supernaturally, that glow for a short while, and then over time, lose the Presence. We are again told that, in this encounter, many saw the actual ring. I say this, as some Saints declare that only they could see the ring, as it lived behind the veil, but was on their finger where a red mark appeared.

In the case of Catherine Of Racconigi (d. 1547), it wasn't Jesus who appeared to her with a ring, it was the Holy Spirit. A Saint had appeared to her when she was young and told her that the Holy Spirit would come upon her in an amazing way. Again, this is not

---

[40] Wiebe, p.85.
[41] Cruz, p.145.

strange when we understand the function of the Great Cloud of Witnesses. We are not told in what form or manifestation the Holy Spirit came, but His voice was heard, and the ring appeared on her finger. This time, it could only be seen by her, and not by others.

> "The espousal took place when three rays of light fell upon her and a heavenly voice sounded; 'I am come to take up my dwelling in you and to cleanse, enlighten, kindle and animate your soul.' After she made a vow of virginity, the mystical espousal took place, and 'the mark of a ring appeared upon her finger.' "[42]

Another Saint, who received a ring that could not be seen, was St Catherine of Siena (d.1380).

But there are a number of accounts of these rings that did manifest through the veil for all to see and hold.

> "St. Veronica Giuliani (d.1727) – A Capuchin nun. The event took place on April 11, 1694. She received a mystical ring from the hand of Jesus which many witnesses were privileged to see. One witness related, "This ring encircled her ring finger as ordinary rings do… This ring was not always viable, but at times was seen clearly."[43]

This espousal didn't just happen to women, but men too, as we are all members of Christ's bride, both male and female. St. Jean Marie Baptiste Vianney (d. 1859) received a ring from Jesus that was clearly witnessed and attested by many.[44]

---

[42] Cruz, p147.
[43] Cruz, p.150.
[44] Cruz, p.150.

St. Colette (d. 1447) not only received a ring from Jesus, but while in deep prayer in the presence of her community, she was drawn into an ecstasy. When she came out of it, she found in her hand a small golden crucifix that had appeared. On one side of the golden crucifix, a blue stone was imprinted, and also a red stone in the middle. Surrounding the red stone, were four pearls fixed, and a larger pearl at the bottom of the cross. These two gifts, the ring and the crucifix, were seen by many.[45]

In my previous book, *Wilderness Like Eden,* I revealed that the Jews are adamant that precious stones fell with the manna in the wilderness. This occurrence is not new, and it clearly has been documented through the history of the Church and of the Saints as well, and shows the union God wants with His bride. These encounters have continued even to the present day. I know of pearls that have manifested from Heaven only a few years ago to some friends of mine.

In 1948 in the ministry of the Golden Candlestick, a group of ladies who spent hours a day in prayer experienced being raptured up into Heavenly encounters, sometimes physically being caught up in their bodies and returning with Heavenly Jewels and gifts of clothing,

> "All the earthly translations and raptures were separate from the translations to heaven, where many would return with sandals entwined with strange jewels, vest-like garments inset with twelve stones representing the tribes of Israel, headdresses arrayed in almost living colours, articles of clothing that would be stitched with

---

[45] Cruz, p.151.

gold thread - I mean the metal, not the colour. These were regular occurrences with the ladies of gold."[46]

These Jewels and gifts were physical, not imaginary, and manifested for them to keep on earth. As I stated earlier, I personally have seen gemstones manifest from Heaven, and I have seen children in Heavenly trances encounter Jesus, and materialise gemstones in their hands, after coming out of their visions. I have also been in the company of children who have brought down Heavenly gifts to give to others, which stay behind the veil. In one occurrence I received a ring and a number of crowns (and other gifts) that were given to me by these children.

Now don't assume that I think I'm super spiritual or a super Saint, we are all receiving gifts from God as we journey with Him, but most don't know of them until they reach Heaven. I could not see the ones the children brought down for me, but I know that they have somehow been fitted into my spiritual armour. I do not know what the function of my ring was, as Scripture lists a number of functions for rings. My ring, I would say, was not connected to the mystical marriage, but was more an impartation of authority, which I have experienced.

As I have seen gemstones manifest and have my own, the fact that this ring and crowns were not physical ones, doesn't mean that they are imagined, as we have seen from the Saints throughout history. Sometimes they stay behind the veil, and sometimes they appear, I have experienced both.

In the book, *Talk With Me In Paradise,* by Angela Curtis, it recounts similar encounters of children bringing down rings,

---

[46] James Maloney, Ladies of Gold; The Remarkable Ministry of the Golden Candlestick, Answering the Cry Publications, 2011, p. 9.

crowns and gifts to give people. It is with these children that I encountered my experiences.

One child shares her experience below; these experiences are full-blown Heaven visitations,

> "There are places in Heaven which are full of royal rings and signet rings, and another is full of crowns for all the children. I can store the treasures Jesus gives me in my house. Sometimes, Jesus gives me a crown to give away to someone. I've given crowns to lots of visitors at our campus. I like giving them to Man and Sir the most. All the crowns have beautiful coloured stones set in the gold, but they all look different. When I put them on someone's head, it gives them peace, and they smile a lot. When I put one on, I feel a buzzing go through me like when the Holy Spirit touches me.
>
> "I've even been given small crowns for the children at the Home (these are the ones that stay behind the veil). I was given a ring, golden clothes and gold sandals for one of the visitors who came to the Home. One day, I was given precious stones to give to Mam. All the gifts in Heaven are glowing with light. I love getting heaven treasure, but I love giving them away more."[47]

What is interesting, is there is a continual trace in history of precious stones and Jewellery from the Old Testament, through the Cross being revealed by Jesus and the Holy Spirit, to the Saints, and even to young children today. Also, the details the child gave about the gifts glowing with light, as St. Catherine dei Ricci also reported, give more confirmation. As does the acknowledgement that some

---

[47] Angela Curtis; Talk With Me In Paradise; Kin & Kingdom Book, 2019, p.87.

rings, crowns, and gifts can be seen, while some cannot be seen by other people.

A personal friend of mine who encounters Heaven often, has received jewellery from the Father, Jesus, and the Holy Spirit. Not only can the Godhead give gifts, but controversial as it might be, those in Heaven can pass on gifts down to the earth. And those on earth who go up can bring down gifts for others on earth for we are one family.

> *"I bow my knees to the Father of our Lord Jesus Christ, from whom the whole family in heaven and earth is named."* (Ephesians 3:14-15).

A word of clarification: as I have read many accounts from Church Saints, often they would encounter Jesus with Angels, the Saints of old, and Mary. I have pondered on this a number of times. Whenever Mary would appear in one of the texts I was reading, I would skip over it and say, "I'm not interested in that one". Then as I reflected more, I have become more at ease with reading Mary in a text, as she is part of the "Great Cloud of Witnesses". BUT – I will not include or accept any vision that Mary appears in teaching false doctrine, or asking to be worshipped or taking part in co-redemption of mankind. But one cannot deny that the "Great Cloud of Witnesses" have appeared throughout history for this is so well documented extensively in the history of the Church.

1 Peter 2:5 says that all Believers are "as living stones", being built into a spiritual house. These symbolisms, these gifts that represent us, these rewards, and marriage unions of rings, are all deeply mystical. We are coming to Him (God) as to a living stone (1 Peter 2:4) to be united as one spirit, and one heart.

I will end this Chapter, with this mystical reality: The Saint Philomena's remains were found in 1802 when workers stumbled over her grave. She was known to have died a martyr, and as the tradition was, a vial of her blood was buried beside her. As this vial of blood was looked at by many Church leaders, a visible chemical reaction happened in the blood, and gems, and flakes of gold and silver appeared in the vial. This substance was chemically tested over forty times and was confirmed to be human blood. Precious stones, rubies and emeralds, pieces of gold and flakes of silver have since appeared mingled with this blood in the vial. This chemical reaction, miracle has been seen many times, and this vial now lives in the Sanctuary of St. Philomena located in Mugnano, Italy.[48]

Even our blood speaks... What are we to make of this? God is more mystical and bigger than our small boxes.

"And there is nothing new under the sun. Is there anything of which it may be said, "See, this is new"? It has already been in ancient times before us." (Ecclesiastes 1:9b,10)

---

[48] Fr. Paul O Sullivan, Saint Philomena; The Wonder Worker, Lisbon; Catholic Printing Press, Rockford, Illinois; Tan, 1993, p.42

CONCLUDING

As we come to the end, I believe I have made an interesting case for reflection. I do not believe I have crossed the line of heresy, but have stretched our understanding of the Godhead. The Godhead is more than an invisible eternal triangle that many Theologians leave us with in their studies.

In our reflection on Granny Rainbow Shekinah, we have seen and covered here, and I have also included new connections,

- The Godhead has an eternal image (form) and likeness, which includes all three members (persons – Father, Son, and Holy Spirit). God is one, but three, a "Oneness" reflected in the three.

- God is identified by the name YHVH (Yahweh), known as the Tetragrammaton. The masculine and feminine elements are perfectly balanced in the Tetragrammaton. The 'yod' has a masculine meaning, the 'he' a feminine one, and the 'vav' a masculine character.

- The Holy Spirit has transcendence over 'all' and is immanent in creation, but is not *of* creation.

- The Holy Spirit, who is God, must be represented on the throne, and identified.

- *"You are clothed with glory and majesty, who cover Yourself with light as with a garment" (Psalm 104:1-2).* The light, veil, mist, robe, is the light of the Holy Spirit (Shekinah).

- The Holy Spirit has a form, a celestial body of glory in Heaven, and can manifest into different representations.

CONCLUDING APPEAL

- ➤ The Holy Spirit's image & likeness incorporates the Rainbow.

- ➤ Hebrews 13:20 speaks of the Trinity's everlasting covenant of redemption. The Rainbow in the sky is a sign (symbol) of this covenant (Genesis 9:16) – drawing attention to how the Holy Spirit, who saves (through the blood of the Son) manifests as a Rainbow (Person).

- ➤ A number of rabbinic sources say that "His Glory" was a divine figure.

- ➤ The Holy Spirit has a theophany (an appearance) that moves behind the veil, and can appear through the veil of the physical world. – A Pillar of a Rainbow etc.

- ➤ The Holy Spirit often veils His face and His facial features to manifest glory.

- ➤ Ruach HaKodesh (Holy Spirit) is a feminine noun in both Hebrew and Aramaic (ruha).

- ➤ In Hebrew, when a noun ends with an 'h' it is almost always a feminine noun. Qesheth means bow (rainbow) in the sky. The word Kabod (glory) means manifestation of God; Chokmah means Wisdom, and Shekinah means dwelling or settling.

- ➤ The Holy Spirit can morph into His celestial body, the Spirit of glory. But also, into a human form (not incarnation).

- ➤ The Holy Spirit, the Spirit of glory, the Shekinah was known by many early Rabbis as one whom sometimes appeared as an old lady or a young bride.

- Sirach 24:15 says, "She (Wisdom) was the smoke of incense in the Tabernacle, her throne in a pillar of clouds."

- Early Rabbis interpreted the book of Song of Solomon as the relationship between God (And Solomon) and His Shekinah, *"Who is She that comes up from the desert like pillars of smoke"* (Song of Solomon 3:6) – (Jubilee Bible).

- *"Set me as a seal on your heart"* (Song of Solomon 8:6) – *"You were sealed with the Holy Spirit"* (Ephesians 1:13).

- Philo referred to the Pillar of Cloud that descended and rested at the entrance of the Tabernacle, as Wisdom. In time, the Pillar of Cloud became known as the Shekinah.

- The Shekinah, the Spirit of Glory was described as Wisdom, Mother Zion, Princess, and Daughter – *"Say to Wisdom, 'You are my sister, and call understanding your nearest kin'."* (Proverbs 7:4)

"All of the glory of the King's daughter is within her, and Her clothing is woven with gold. She shall be brought to the King in robes of many colours." (Psalm 45:13-14).

An interesting thought is that, if Granny Rainbow (in morph form) walked on the earth, she would be in our perception, like a sister, as Jesus is like our brother (Hebrews 2:11). He is not ashamed to call us his brothers and sisters, yet while still being God.

- Early Jewish and Christian Church Fathers attributed a feminine aspect, and character to the Holy Spirit. I will admit not many, but some did, and none were Gnostics or heretics.

- Jesus said, he and his cousins, John the Baptist were both her Children (Wisdom) *"The Son of Man has come eating and drinking, and you say, Look, a glutton and a winebibber, a friend of tax collectors and sinners! But Wisdom is justified by all her children"* (Luke 7:34-35).

- "As a Mother, the Spirit of Wisdom sanctifies each member of the Church, nourishing them with the bread of life, supporting them, until finally she clothes them in a robe of glory" (Neil Weber)

- *"Jesus grew strong in Spirit and was filled with Wisdom,"* (Luke 2:40).

- Jesus spoke of wanting to gather his children, through the drawing of the Spirit, as a hen gathers her chicks under her wings (Matt 23:37)

- Jesus instructed Nicodemus that the Holy Spirit was like a womb of which one must be born from (John 3:6).

- *"...and the Spirit (feminine) of God was hovering over the face of the waters"* (Genesis 1:2)

  "As an eagle stirs up its nest, hovers over its young" (Deuteronomy 32:11) God leads His people.

- *"She is Tree of Life to those who take hold of her..."* (Proverbs 3:18)

  "If any man would come after me, let him take hold of his cross, and follow me." (Matthew 16:24) – the spirit of eternal life brings forth the fruit of salvation.

- The formation of Eve, coming forth from her Adam, is like the procession of the Spirit from God. Our Lord gave his life so the Spirit could come down, surrounded by fire, and enter the Church. The mystical body of Christ, the new Adam, received a new Helper; the Holy Spirit, like Eve.

- There was a certain man called Simon, who tried to buy the Holy Spirit as if the Spirit was a harlot. Peter said, may your silver perish with you (Acts 8:18-20). Wisdom cannot be bought with the finest gold, nor can her price be weighed out in silver. She cannot be bought. (Job 28:15-19)

- "She dwells in the Church, bringing out her own image, that the Church may be like her, a radiant bride, without stain or flaw or any such thing, but holy and faultless, a pure virgin for Christ." (Neil Weber).

- *"So, God created man in His image; in the image of God He created him; male and female He created them" (Genesis 1:27).*

- The family on earth is a picture/representation of the Godhead "family" so to speak. Father, Holy Spirit ('wife'), Son; and we (Born Again Believers) are adopted children into that family. This is why Satan is so desperate to break up marriages and families here on earth because they are the image of God! (Colleen Kaluza)

- "The Spirit of Wisdom is the mirror of God's majesty… And the man called his wife's name Eve because she was the mother of all the living. The word 'Eve' means Life. Of all that she is, she is most of all life. She is the mirror of Wisdom, God's life giving breath. From the creation of the world, the invisible things of God, his eternal power and divinity, are clearly visible through the things he has made." (Neil Weber)

- I quote another two early Church Fathers not mentioned so far, who are bold in their assertions. The Church Father Epiphanius (315-430), Bishop of Salamis said, "And the Holy Spirit is to be like Christ, but she is a female being" (Epiphanius, Panarion 19,4, 1-2) and the Church Father Hippolytus (170-236), a Christian Presbyter of Rome said, "The male is the Son of God, and the female is called the Holy Spirit" (Hippolytus, Refutatio 9, 13, 3).

- This does not mean I'm stating that God the Holy Spirit is a woman or is female, but just as Jesus could morph in disguised forms, so can the Holy Spirit.

- Origen, Cyril of Alexandria, Gregory of Nyssa, Augustine and others, have interpreted Genesis 18 to be the Trinity (Father, Son and Holy Spirit) manifesting as 3 men.

- Under NO circumstances does the interpretation given in this book reflect, in philosophy, worldview or theology, Gnostic beliefs of the *goddess* Sophia.

- Some early Church Saints experienced a lady appearing out of a cloud (Cloud symbol of the Holy Spirit) on earth, and similar rescues from this lady.

- The Jews wrote a lot of Wisdom literature about this appearing lady. The Catholic Church canonised the Book of Wisdom about her in the Old Testament. The Orthodox liturgy calls upon her, before each Gospel is read aloud, 'Sophia' (Σοφία - Greek for 'Wisdom', **not** to be confused with the previous mention of the *goddess* Sophia).

- The Bishop Martyrius (6th Century), said Believers are as one 'who has been held worthy of the hovering of the Holy

Spirit, who, like a mother hovers over us as she gives sanctification, and through her hovering over us, we are made worthy of sonship.'

- Nicolaus Zinzendorf, Theologian, Bishop of the Moravian Church (18th Century), believed the term "Mother" best described the nature (not gender) of the Holy Spirit.

- John Crowder in his book, *The ecstasy of loving God,* says, "The Holy Spirit, is of course, the Spirit of Wisdom."

- I have documented modern (recent) accounts of encountering the Holy Spirit in human likeness (not incarnation, but morphed) – Granny Rainbow!

- I have shown the mystical marriage and gifts that can be received from the Godhead throughout history.

The Holy Spirit longs to have deep fellowship with us, and communion. The Holy Spirit is closer than we think, walking among us, longing for us to dine and with Him, and drink the wine and eat the bread of the Godhead and be filled with Wisdom and Joy.

> *"Therefore, if there is any consolation in Christ, if any comfort of love, if any fellowship of the Spirit…" (Philippians 2:1)*

> *"The Grace of the Lord Jesus Christ, and the love of God, and the communion of the Holy Spirit, be with you all, Amen." (2 Corinthians 13:14)*

Throughout this book I have not stated that the Holy Spirit is female or a woman. My Thesis is that the Holy Spirit *can morph* into human likeness, of which is often in *female form*. I document other thinkers who refer to the Holy Spirit as female, so that one cannot accuse me of pulling an idea out of my head, which in fact has Jewish roots, of which I stop at: The Holy Spirit can morph, but *is not* female.

I say the Holy Spirit has the *DNA* of both male and female. I don't believe there are two males and one female in the Trinity, but one 'being' who is three persons, who has both the DNA of male and female in their image. All members have this DNA, of which they can choose how they express those attributes/natures.

Who is Lady Wisdom? This is an interesting question, and one that others can research and study. But as we come to the end, I will leave us with these references,

> *"Wisdom has built her house. She has hewn out her seven pillars; She has slaughtered her meat; She has mixed her wine, She has furnished her table, She has sent out maidens, She cries out from the highest places of the city, 'whoever is simple, let him turn in here'. As for him who lacks understanding, 'Come, eat of my bread, and drink of the wine I have mixed. Forsake foolishness and live, and go in the way of understanding...'" "The fear of the Lord is the beginning of Wisdom, and the knowledge of the Holy One, is understanding. For by me your days will be multiplied, and years of life will be added to you." (Proverbs 9:1-6, 10-11)*

> *"I learned both what is secret and what is manifest, for Wisdom, the fashioner of all things taught me. For there is in her a spirit; intelligent, holy, unique, manifold, subtle, mobile, clear, unpolluted, distinct, invulnerable, loving the good, keen, irresistible, beneficent, humane, steadfast, sure, free from anxiety, all-powerful, overseeing all, and penetrating through the spirits that are intelligent, pure, and altogether subtle. For Wisdom is*

more mobile than any notion, she pervades/penetrates all things because of purity. For she is a breath of the power of God, and a pure emanation of the glory of the almighty; therefore, nothing defiled gains entrance into her. For she is a reflection of eternal light, a spotless mirror of the working of God; and an image of his goodness. Although but one, she can do all things; and while remaining in herself, she renews all things; in every generation she passes into holy souls and makes them friends of God, and prophets. For God loves nothing so much as the person who lives with Wisdom." (Wisdom of Solomon 7:21-28)

"Send her forth from the holy heavens, and from the throne of your glory, send her that she may labour at my side, and that I may learn what is pleasing to you." (Wisdom of Solomon 9:10).

So, keep your eyes open, and be ready to meet and fellowship with Granny Rainbow Shekinah! For the pure in heart shall see God.

REFLECTIVE
Scriptures

A quick list of some major referenced Scriptures on taking on different "forms", genders, and morphing!

> *"After that, He appeared in another 'form' to two of them as they walked and went into the country." (Mark 16:12)*

> *"Now behold, two of them were travelling that same day to a village called Emmaus, which was seven miles from Jerusalem. And as they talked together of all these things which had happened. So it was, while they conversed and reasoned that Jesus himself drew near and went with them. But their eyes were restrained, so that they did not know Him… Then they drew near the village where they were going, and He indicated that He would have gone farther. But they constrained Him, saying, 'Abide with us, for it is toward evening, and the day is far spent.' And He went in to stay with them. Now it came to pass, as He sat at the table with them, that He took bread, blessed and broke it, and gave it to them. Then their eyes were opened, and they knew Him; and He vanished from their sight." (Luke 24:13-16 -28-31)*

> *"Now when she had said this, she turned around and saw Jesus standing there, and did not know that it was Jesus. Jesus said to her, Woman why are you weeping? Whom are you seeking? She, supposing Him to be the gardener, said to Him, Sir, if you have carried Him away, tell me where you have laid Him, and I will take Him way." (John 20:14-15)*

> *"And the Holy Spirit descended in bodily form like a dove upon Him, and a voice came from heaven which said, 'You are My beloved Son, in You I am well pleased'." (Luke 3:22)*

> *"He stretched out the form of a hand, and took me by a lock of my hair; and the Spirit lifted me up between earth and heaven."* (Ezekiel 8:3)

> *"The Spirit of God has made me, and the breath of the Almighty gives me life"* (Job 33:4)

> *"Your hands have made me and fashioned me…"* (Psalm 119:73)

If the Spirit formed mankind, then I think it is not hard to think He can morph into that image, which reflects the image of God. There is extensive rabbinic tradition that God uses His hands to create.[49]

To reject Anthropomorphic images of God, means Moses didn't see God's feet on a pavement of sapphire stone. God didn't hand Moses tablets written by His finger, that God had no face to hide, when Moses asked to see it, and that God doesn't mount on a Cherub…

> *"Then I will take away my hand, and you shall see My back, but My face shall not be seen"* (Exodus 33:23)

There are three parables in the Gospel of Luke, where God reveals himself as the Father looking out for his prodigal son, the good Shepherd who finds his lost sheep, and the Woman who finds her lost coin. These Parables teach that God seeks to save and encourage those who are feeling afar. Parables are not meant to be interpreted word for word as literal, but God is a Father, Jesus is a shepherd who seeks his sheep (believers), and the Woman seeks to find lost souls (coins).

---

[49] Avot de-Rbbi Natan 1; Shloyshe Sheorim; Hekhalot Rabbati 10.

> *"What Woman having ten silver coins, if she may lose one, does not light a lamp, and sweep the house, and carefully seek till she may find it." (Luke 15:8)*

In the book of Proverbs, the woman Wisdom is walking the streets, and says she will pour out her spirit on you. This is the same spirit, the Holy Spirit, that Acts 2:17 speaks of: *"And it shall come to pass in the last days, says God, that I will pour out my Spirit on all flesh..."* The Holy Spirit can dwell with us, on us, and in us.

> *"Wisdom cries aloud in the streets, she lifts up her voice in the broad places; she calls at the head of the bustling corners, at the entrances of the gates, in the city, she offers words. Turn at my reproof, behold I will pour out my spirit on you." (Proverbs 1:20,21,23)*

> *"He who finds me, finds life, and wins favour from the Lord. But he who sins against me wounds his own soul. All who hate me love death." (Proverbs 8:35-36)*

> *"And I will pray the Father, and He will give you another Helper, that he may abide with you forever, "the Spirit of truth, whom the world cannot receive, because it neither sees Him nor knows Him; but you know Him, for He dwells with you and will be in you. "I will not leave you orphans; I will come to you." (John 14:16-18).*

> *"Let brotherly love continue. Do not forget to entertain strangers, for by so doing some have unwittingly entertained <u>"angels"</u> (Greek word, messenger or agent of change)" (Hebrews 13:1).*

Many Theologians have seen a connection between the mysterious Queen of Sheba (1 Kings 10) and Wisdom (Holy Spirit).

She comes to Solomon's temple with spices, gold and precious stones, and to check he has applied her wisdom,

> *"Wisdom has built herself a house, she has carved her seven pillars. She has prepared her food, spiced her wine, and she has set her table." (Proverbs 9:1-2)*

> *"By Wisdom a house is built, by understanding it is made secure and by knowledge its rooms are filled with all kinds of costly and precious stones." (Proverbs 24:3-4).*

Have we limited Him? He radiates like a swirl of coloured mist around the Father on the throne, like a veil of glory. He moves like a coloured Pillar in the heavens, He hovered over creation, and was breathed out into Adam's body, shining through him like a garment of light. He manifested as a Pillar of a Cloud, and a Pillar of Fire. He morphed into a 'bodily form' like a dove over Jesus at his baptism. He dwells in us – our bodies are His Temple, and dances on our heads like a flame. He is transcendent over and immanent in creation. If He is like the "Image" and "Likeness" of the other two members of the Godhead, for He is God, then He has the same or similar abilities, unless you believe He is less. He is the Master Morpher, and there is more to His personality, few have seen. How close can He come? For He will not let you be an Orphan.

BIBLIOGRAPHY

Allison, Gregg R. (2011) *Historical Theology; An Introduction to Christian Doctrine,* Zondervan Publishers.

Arns, David M. (2014) *Gold Dust, Jewels, and More Manifestations of God?,* Createspace Independent Publishing Platform.

Bercot, David W. (1998) *A Dictionary of Early Christian Beliefs,* Hendrickson Publishers, Inc.

Bird, Michael F. (2014) *How God Became Jesus: The Real Origins of Belief in Jesus' Divine Nature,* Zondervan Publishers.

Boshoff, Pastor Rudolph P. (January 2016) *Divine Prefigurements in the Early Jewish Understanding of Yahweh,* referenced from https://adlucem.co/divine-prefigurements-in-the-early-jewish-understanding-of-yahweh-by-rudolph-p-boshoff/ accessed November 2019

Bregman, Marc, *Ruach Ha-Qodesh* (The Holy Spirit), Unpublished.

Bundesen, Lynne. (2019) *The Feminine Spirit at the Heart of the Bible,* Anamchara Books.

Cruz, Joan Carroll. (1997) *Mysteries Marvels & Miracles: In the Lives Of The Saints,* Tan Books & Publishers Inc.

Curtis, Angela. (2019) *Talk With Me In Paradise,* Kin & Kingdoms Books Publishers.

Doles, Jeff. (2008) *Miracles & Manifestations of the Holy Spirit in the History of the Church,* Walking Barefoot Ministries Publishers.

Dye, Dinah. (2016) *The Temple Revealed In Creation,* Foundations in Torah Publishing.

Esther, Gulshan (1992) *The Torn Veil; The Story of Sister Gulshan Esther, as told to Thelma Sangster,* Marshall Pickering.

Frame, John M. (2002) *The Doctrine of God,* P&R Publishers Co.

Fee, Gordon D. (2007) *Pauline Christology, An Exegetical-Theological Study,* Hendrickson Publishers.

Fellows, Richard. (2019) *Wilderness Like Eden,* WordWyze Publishing.

Fishbane, Michael *Some Forms of Divine Appearance in Ancient Jewish Thought.* (In '*From Ancient Israel to modern Judaism*'. Ed. Jacob Neusner. Atlanta: Scholar's Press, p. 261-270)

Geisler, Norman L. (2003) *Systematic Theology, Volume Two – God/Creation,* Bethany House Publishers.

Goshen-Gottstein, Alon. (1994) *The Body as image of God in Rabbinic Literature.* (Harvard Theological Review 8:7 p. 171-195)

Hamilton, James M. Jr. (2006) *God's Indwelling Presence, The Holy Spirit in The Old & New Testament,* Broadman & Holman Publishers.

Heisler, Michael S. (2015) *The Unseen Realm, Recovering the supernatural worldview of the Bible,* Faithlife Publishers.

Ireland, Michael, *Miraculously Delivered by God, Unable to read Bible.* 2019 https://www.assistnews.net/miraculously-delivered-by-god-unable-to-read-his-word/

Johnson, Ian (2012) *Israel, God and the ANZACs,* His Amazing Glory Ministries.

Kendall, R.T. (2014) *Holy Fire: A Balanced, Biblical Look At The Holy Spirit's Work in Our Lives,* Charisma House Publishers.

Maloney, James. (2011) *Ladies of Gold: The Remarkable Ministry of The Golden Candlestick,* Answering the Cry Publications.

Martin, Walter. (2003) *The Kingdom of The Cults,* Bethany House Publishers.

Marmorstein, Arthur. (1950) *The Holy Spirit in Rabbinic Legend,* London Oxford Publishers.

Mason, Phil. (2010) *Quantum Glory, The Science of Heaven Invading Earth,* XP Publishing.

Mother Teresa (1975) *A Gift for God,* Fount Paperback.

Packer, Lyn. (2010) *Visions, Visitations & the Voice of God,* XP Publishing.

Parson, Mike. (2018) *My Journey Beyond Beyond,* The Choir Press.

Ware, Bruce A. (2005) *Father, Son, and Holy Spirit, Relationships, Roles & Relevance.* CrossWay Books.

Weber, Neil Anthony. (2016) *Who is Sophia: Getting to know the Spirit of Wisdom in 50 Days,* Independent publishing.

Weber, Neil Anthony. (2018) *Sophia in the Desert: 40 Days with Wisdom,* Independent publishing.

White, James R. (1998) *The Forgotten Trinity: Recovering the Heart of Christian Belief,* Bethany House Publishers.

Wiebe, Phillip H. (2014) *Visions and Appearances Of Jesus*, ACU Press / Leafwood Publishers.

Reymond, Robert L. (1998) *A New Systematic Theology of The Christian Faith*, Thomas Nelson Publishers.

Rowe, Peter. (1996) *Explaining The Presence of God*, Sovereign World publishers.

Schäfer, Peter. (2004) *Mirror of His Beauty: Feminine Images of God from the Bible to the early Kabbalah*, Princeton University Press.

Schwartz, Howard. (2004) *Tree of Souls: Mythology Of Judaism*, Oxford University Press.

Shapiro, Rami. (2005) *The Divine Feminine in Biblical Wisdom Literature*, Jewish Lights Publishing.

Smith, Ralph A. (2004) *Trinity & Reality: An Introduction to the Christian Faith*, Canon Press.

St. Martin of Tours – there are many resources on the internet, with varying details. One I quoted part of, is from https://jesusthrumary.blogspot.com/2011/11/nov-11-2011-friday-st-martin-of-tours.html

Teresa, Mother. (1975) *A Gift for God*, Harper Collins Publishers.

Woodworth-Etter, Maria. (1981) *A Diary of Signs and Wonders*, Harrison House.

Young, William Paul. (2007) *The Shack, Where Tragedy confronts Eternity*, Hachette Book Group USA.

NOTES

If you've enjoyed this book, be sure to get hold of Richard Fellow's first book, *Wilderness Like Eden*, published mid-2019.

ISBN 978-0-648-58830-6 Available at all online bookstores worldwide, or direct from author – richfellows@hotmail.com

www.ingramcontent.com/pod-product-compliance
Lightning Source LLC
Chambersburg PA
CBHW030258010526
44107CB00053B/1753